Bible Fun Stuff

FOR 2ND-3RD GRADES

Pretty

Quick & easy

Bible Dramas

David C. Cook
transforming lives together

PRETTY QUICK & EASY BIBLE DRAMAS
Published by David C. Cook
4050 Lee Vance View
Colorado Springs, CO 80918 U.S.A.

David C. Cook Distribution Canada
55 Woodslee Avenue, Paris, Ontario, Canada N3L 3E5

David C. Cook U.K., Kingsway Communications
Eastbourne, East Sussex BN23 6NT, England

David C. Cook and the graphic circle C logo
are registered trademarks of Cook Communications Ministries.

Written by Sheila Seifert
Cover Design by BMB Design
Cover Photography © Brad Armstrong Photography
Interior Design by Rebekah Lyon
Interior Illustrations by Phyllis Cahill

ISBN 978-1-4347-6860-5

First Printing 2008
Printed in the United States

1 2 3 4 5 6 7 8 9 10

FOR 2ND-3RD GRADES
Pretty
Quick & easy
BiBLe DRamas

Table of Contents

Introduction

The stories of Scripture are full of drama, suspense, humor, human frailty, tragedy, and triumph. These stories and the truths they hold become anchored in our hearts and minds when they are combined with fun, movement, and imagination. These dramatic activities are designed to help students think and explore the Bible in new ways, enabling them to personalize their faith.

Pretty Quick & Easy Bible Dramas is crammed full of active and imaginative explorations of Bible truths. Most require only a few props and a simple set. Get ready to teach your students by starting with the **Bible Background** at the beginning of each lesson. Take a few minutes to put yourself inside the story and ask what God wants to teach you personally. Then turn to the next page for a **Summary** of the activity, the **Setting**, some easy **Teacher Tips** to enrich learning and a simple list of **Props** and **Characters**. The scripts you'll find in this book make great readers' theater events, or you can rehearse, memorize lines, and stage full productions. Invite other classes or adult groups from your congregation to be the audience or the actors.

You can use these activities in any order. Adapt them to your space and time availability. These drama activities can be an optional supplement to David C. Cook's *Bible-in-Life* or *Echoes* curriculum—or any curriculum for that matter. Use the **Correlation Chart** on page 112 to match a drama to a lesson. Or use the **Scripture** or **Topic Index** at the back of the book to match up an activity to a Bible story you're studying with your students, and let the drama add unexpected excitement to your learning time.

You can also use a script or activity as the core of your learning time. Take a few minutes to look up the Bible Background and review the Bible story together. Then follow the simple directions for the script or activity to explore the Bible truth the story teaches. Any directions you need to speak directly to your students are in bold.

At the end of each script or activity, you'll find **Curtain Call.** This part of the lesson suggests some discussion questions that will help students process and apply the Bible truth of the story. Curtain Call doesn't have to take a long time, but use these few minutes to help your students solidify the lesson focus.

Options for Using the Dramas

You might use these dramas with kids from your class playing the parts. Or you could recruit actors from the youth group or from adult assistant teachers in your Sunday school program. Whichever actors you choose, plan to photocopy the skit for each character and highlight each character's part. If at all possible, give your actors the skits far enough in advance so that they can read over their parts and then at least walk through the action together.

For all of your actors, encourage them to be dramatic, adding hand motions and movement. Have them think through the different lines and see if a melodramatic flair or a facial expression would express the feeling of their lines. Help them feel comfortable in the spotlight. Now, dive in for fun, surprise, and lots of laughter. Set your imagination free and get ready to romp through the Bible in a whole new way!

Hide and Seek

Through a game of hide and seek, the kids learn that God can always see them.

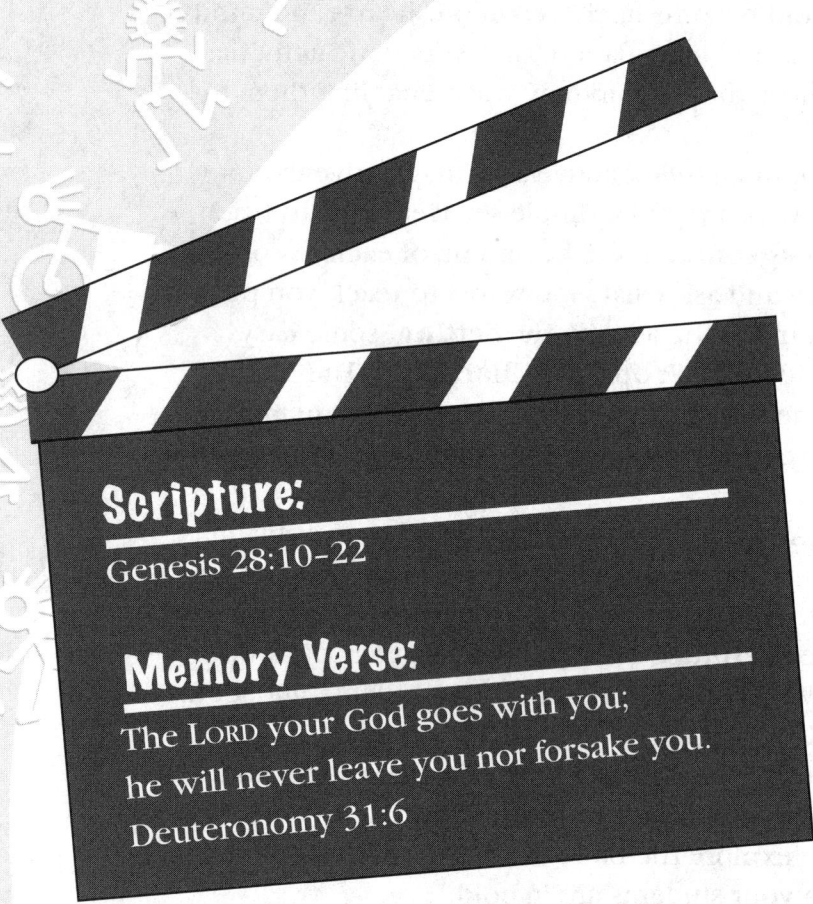

Scripture:

Genesis 28:10–22

Memory Verse:

The LORD your God goes with you;
he will never leave you nor forsake you.
Deuteronomy 31:6

Bible Background

Jacob was running from an angry brother. He knew he didn't deserve God's help, much less His blessing. Yet the trick he played to get a blessing, though misguided, contained a mixed motivation. Unworthy as Jacob was, he showed a hunger to know God. The birthright Jacob sought from Esau (Gen. 25:31) did not revolve around inheritance of money, but rather it meant the headship of the family in its covenant with God. Esau valued the things of this world, but Jacob wanted divine blessings.

In spite of Jacob's deceit, and now fear and homelessness, communication between God and His people was not broken. This was the God of Abraham and Isaac, Jacob's father and grandfather, and now He would be the God of Jacob as well. The shining stairway in Jacob's dream confirmed God's desire to accept and use Jacob.

Jesus mentioned Jacob's vision, inserting Himself in place of the Genesis ladder: "You shall see . . . the angels of God ascending and descending on [not the ladder, but] the Son of Man" (John 1:51). Jesus is our ladder to God; He provides a modern-day Bethel.

Have you ever felt like Jacob—alone, afraid, and seemingly far from God? We can take heart in Jacob's experience and know that in the middle of our sin comes God's saving revelation of Himself. God has promised that He will be with us (Isa. 41:10).

Summary:

A class wants to play hide and seek with God. After each time the kids hide, the question is asked, "Can God see us now?" By the end of the game, the students conclude that playing hide and seek with God is a bad idea—because God always wins! The teacher points out that it's a good thing they can't hide from God. No matter where they go or what trouble they get into, they'll always know that God is there.

Setting: A Sunday school classroom

Props:

■ Desks or chairs

Characters:

■ Jevan
■ Teacher
■ Class (any number of kids)

Teacher Tip:

Any number of furniture props can be used for this skit. Just adapt the stage setting to whatever you have handy in your classroom.

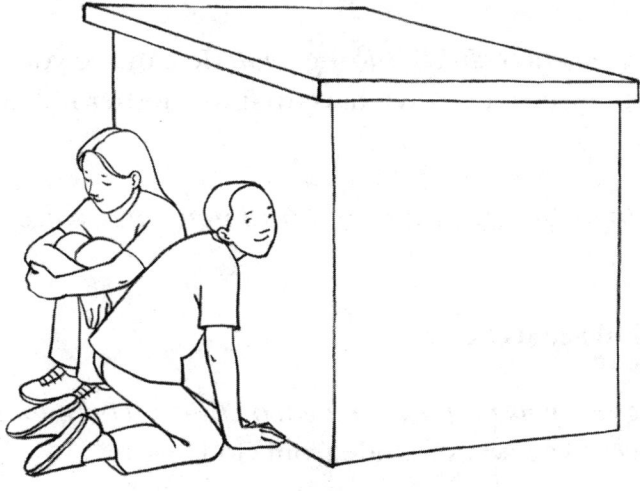

Hide and Seek

*As the scene opens, the **Teacher** is at the front of the class. **Jevan** and the rest of the class sit in student chairs.*

Teacher: We have a few minutes left at the end of class. What game should we play?

Class: Hide and seek!

Teacher: Who wants to be It?

Jevan: We all want to hide, so God can be It.

Class: Yeah!

Teacher: It's hard to hide from God.

Jevan: We're good at hiding.

Teacher: Okay. Everyone should find a hiding place. And then, Jevan, you can ask, "Can God see us now?"

Jevan: Okay.

Teacher: Then I'll let you know if God can still see you. Are you ready?

Class: Ready!

Teacher: Are you set?

Class: Set!

Teacher: Then you'd better go and find hiding places.

*(**Jevan** and the **class** go and hide.)*

Jevan: *(Calls out.)* Can God see us now?

Teacher: Yes, He can! *(Name each child's hiding spot:* He can see you under the table, behind the bookcase, near the closet, etc.) You'll have to find another hiding place if you want to hide from God.

*(The **class** comes out of their hiding places and find new ones. Once everyone is hidden, **Jevan** asks his question again.)*

Jevan: *(Calls out.)* Can God see us now?

Teacher: Yes, He can! *(Again, you might name each child's whereabouts.)* You'll have to find a more secret hiding place if you want to hide from God.

Jevan: God is good at hide and seek.

Teacher: Yes, He is.

*(The **kids** find other hiding spots. When all are hidden, **Jevan** asks his question.)*

Jevan: Can God see us now?

Teacher: Yes, He can! *(Again, you may name each child's location.)* You'll have to find a sneakier hiding place if you want to hide from God.

*(Have **students** come out of their hiding places.)*

Jevan: God is too good at this game. We've hidden everywhere we can in this room, and He still found us.

Teacher: God can find you in this room, in our city, in our state, and in our country.

Jevan: Can He find us if we go to another continent or into outer space?

Teacher: Yes, He can. God is so good at hide and seek that He can find you no matter where you go.

Jevan: That's nice that we can't get lost from Him!

Teacher: No matter how far you travel or how much trouble you get into or how many mistakes you make or how hard your life is, God still knows your name and knows where you are. You are special to Him, and nothing can change that. God is with you wherever you go.

Curtain Call

■ **Have you ever felt far from God or alone or afraid like Jacob?**

■ **Where could God see you in our classroom?** *(everywhere!)* **Can you name some places where you could go to get away from God?** *(There isn't any place at all on earth or in our universe.)*

■ **What are things you might do or that might happen to you that God wouldn't know about?** *(nothing at all. He knows and sees absolutely everything.)*

■ **How do you feel knowing that God always stays with you, no matter what?** *(Let volunteers share—they might say safe, happy, peaceful, or sometimes even a little uncomfortable because they can't get away with anything!)*

Marble Clues

A boy learns that following directions—or not—shows what he really wants.

Scripture:

1 Samuel 8—10

Memory Verse:

Choose for yourselves this day whom you will serve.

Joshua 24:15

Bible Background

The people of Israel had been led by judges and, most recently, by the prophet, Samuel. They knew Samuel was getting old and that his sons did not obey God. They truly had a need for new leadership, and they went about it in the right way by consulting God on the matter. But one thing they didn't do right—they made demands of God rather than wait for His direction.

The Israelites' request for a king seemed reasonable. Having a human king was a workable plan. Moses had even written instructions about when Israel would have a king. While the Lord had made provision for such a time, He knew that in this case, they simply wanted to be like their heathen neighbors. He knew that the people of Israel were in fact rejecting His leadership.

Despite the Lord's clear answer through Samuel, the people decided to go their own way. Even then, God stepped in to help them: He chose their king. God is gracious and forgiving even when we sin.

How often do we go to God with a reasonable request? Our problem isn't that our requests are necessarily bad. It's that we need to be willing to hear and accept God's answer rather than demanding that He gives us the answer we want to hear. "In his heart a man plans his course, but the LORD determines his steps" (Prov. 16:9). Allow God to speak to your heart in whatever requests you are bringing to Him today, and be willing to obey His guidance.

Summary:

In order to play the class marble game, Travis, Alesha, William, and Nikki must follow their teacher's directions to find their assigned marbles. When Travis rejects the directions and does his own thing, he finds that he's the one who loses out.

Setting: A classroom party

Props:

- Four sheets of paper with writing on them
- A teacher's desk
- Four marbles—yellow, black, green, and red or orange—or any four colors you choose—placed around the room. The yellow should be on the floor at the back classroom wall, the black one on the floor by the left wall, the green one on the floor by the right wall, and the red-orange one under the teacher's desk.

Characters:

- Travis
- William
- Nikki
- Alesha

Teacher Tip:

If your stage area doesn't have walls to place the marbles by, substitute students' desks or chairs, and change the dialogue and action appropriately. If Travis doesn't have a wall to lean against, he might sit on a table.

Marble Clues

*As the scene opens, **Travis**, **Alesha**, **William**, and **Nikki** each hold a sheet of paper and pretend to silently read.*

Travis: *(Looks up from his paper.)* I don't feel like reading all this. Just tell me what it says.

Alesha: *(Reading from her paper.)* Your teacher has given you clues so you can find a marble and play in the all-class marble game. Each student has been given different clues.

Travis: *(Shrugs.)* Not that different. *(**Travis** tries to peek at **William**'s directions.)*

William: Read your own. Mine won't help you. We each have to find our own marble.

*(**William**, **Alesha**, and **Nikki** walk 10 paces ahead, counting quietly but so that the audience can hear them. **Travis** follows them.)*

Travis: This is great. So far so good.

Alesha: Are you reading your own clues?

Travis: *(Holds his directions in front of his face.)* Did you say something?

*(**William**, **Alesha**, and **Nikki** turn around three times, counting each turn out loud. **Travis** peeks out from behind his paper and randomly spins around.)*

Travis: Our clues seem pretty similar so far.

*(**Travis** turns away and feigns interest in something unrelated. **William** walks to the left classroom wall, **Alesha** to the right, and **Nikki** to the back. When **Travis** finally notices, he walks toward **William**, then **Alesha**, and then **Nikki**, as if he can't decide which way to go. He ends up walking to the front classroom wall. **William**, **Alesha**, and **Nikki** look around for their marbles. **Travis** leans against a wall, watching them.)*

Nikki: I found it! Mine's a lemon-drop marble.

William: Here's mine. It's glossy black. Just the one I wanted.

Alesha: Mine wasn't hard to find either. It's light green—one of my favorite colors.

William: How's your search going, Travis?

Travis: Nothing so far. I need help.

William, Alesha, and Nikki: I'll help. *(They search the floor by the wall where Travis is relaxing.)*

William: Your marble isn't here.

Travis: It has to be. This is where my directions led me.

Nikki: Are you sure? Let me see your paper.

*(**Nikki** takes the directions from **Travis**. **Alesha** hurries over to look too. **William** keeps searching.)*

Nikki: Travis, you're nowhere close to your marble. Did you even read your clues?

Travis: *(Shrugs.)* So I chose not to. I decided to go with my instincts.

Nikki: If you don't care about finding your marble, then I don't either. *(**Nikki** hands back the paper.)*

Travis: But I do care. I just figured I could find it on my own.

Nikki: Your choices show whether you care or not.

Alesha: And if you choose not to follow our teacher's directions, you can't play marbles with us.

Nikki: Your choice. *(**Alesha** and **Nikki** exit.)*

Travis: Why do I have to do it the teacher's way?

William: Because if you don't, you won't find your marble. She hid it, so only she knows where it is. Remember what we learned in Sunday school? If you want to follow God, you show it by what you choose to do—like reading your Bible or being kind when you don't feel like it. What you choose to do matters. I hope you follow the clues the teacher wrote for you. I don't want to be the only guy playing marbles. *(**William** exits.)*

Travis: *(Sighs.)* Oh, okay. I can't believe I have to do everything the teacher's way, but I really want to play marbles with my friends. *(**Travis** picks up his directions. His lips move as if he's reading. He walks 10 paces, reads, turns in a circle three times, reads, and walks to the teacher's desk, where he finds his marble under it.)* My choices really do make a difference. What a great marble! *(Yells to characters offstage.)* Wait up! I found it. I'll take you all on. *(**Travis** exits.)*

Curtain Call

■ **Do you think it was wrong for the Israelites to ask for a king? Why or why not?** *(It wasn't wrong to ask, but they had the wrong motives when they asked.)*

■ **What was the difference in the way Nikki, Alesha, and William searched for clues and the way Travis did it?** *(The first three followed the teacher's directions and found their marbles right away, but Travis didn't and so couldn't find his marble.)*

■ **How do we follow God's directions?** *(by doing what the Bible teaches, by doing what we know is right, by obeying the people God put in our lives to lead us, etc.)*

■ **What are some choices you could make this week to show that you follow God?** *(Let volunteers share, encouraging them to be specific and realistic for their age: read the Bible, let someone else go first in line, tell someone about Jesus, share with my brother or sister, etc.)*

Number Two

Through losing a race, a girl learns that jealousy prevents us from being grateful.

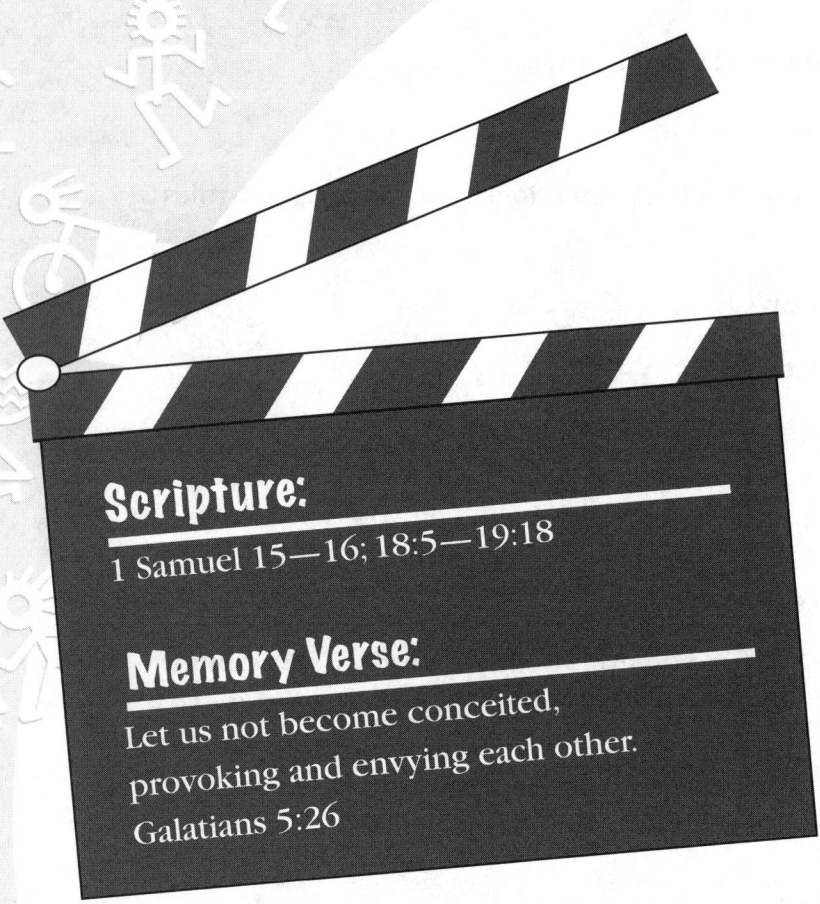

Scripture:
1 Samuel 15—16; 18:5—19:18

Memory Verse:
Let us not become conceited, provoking and envying each other.
Galatians 5:26

Bible Background

The Amalekites were a ruthless and cruel neighbor of Israel. God intended to punish the Amalekites for their unrelenting attacks on His people (Exod. 17:8; 1 Sam. 15:2), and He told Saul to totally destroy them—even none of their possessions were to be spared. Saul, however, kept alive the Amalekite king and the best of the livestock. When Samuel confronted him, Saul cast the blame on others (1 Sam. 15:20-21). As a result, God took the kingship away from Saul—along with His Spirit.

Then God chose a man after His own heart to be the next king. Though Saul didn't know yet that God had chosen a simple shepherd and musician named David to succeed him, Saul had noticed David. Saul discerned David's heart for God, his courage, his growing leadership skills, and his resultant popularity. As a result, Saul felt threatened.

Feelings of jealousy do not necessarily arise out of not having what we want. Saul was powerful, rich, handsome, popular, and successful. Yet he felt insecure and feared someone who had less than him.

David was the one who had a right to feel jealous. He had been promised the kingship by God but instead was forced to flee for his life, abandoning his friends and family, and living in the desert for years. David's response was to cry out to God continually (as shown in the psalms) and to be thankful for all that God had given him. A good response to envy and jealousy is thanksgiving and trusting in God.

Summary:

When Abby's class wins a kickball game against the fifth grade team, she is so filled with jealousy over Gina scoring the winning goal that she can't do the victory chant with her class. With Devon's help, Abby chooses to release her jealousy, trust God, and not take matters into her own hands, as King Saul did with David.

Setting: A school playground

Props:

None
(Optional) **kickball that students can toss around while chanting**

Characters:

- **Abby**
- **Devon**
- **Gina**
- **Class (can be a few or several children)**

Teacher Tip:

So that the audience can clearly see and hear, position the main characters at the front of the stage area, facing front, and have the rest of the characters (the students) behind them.

Number Two

As the scene opens, a group of students and **Devon** *are jumping up and down, arms raised and pointing up to show they are number one.* **Abby** *stands a few steps away.*

Class: *(Chanting.)* We're number one! We're number one!

Devon: Abby, join us.

Abby: I can't. I'm not number one.

Devon: What do you mean? Our kickball team won against the fifth-grade team. That's never happened at our school. Everyone in our class is number one today.

Class: We're number one! We're number one!

*(***Gina** *enters, and the class crowds around congratulating her, patting her on the back, giving high-fives, and so on.)*

Abby: I told you, I'm not number one. *(Points at* **Gina***.)* Gina's number one.

Devon: Gina? You mean because she scored the winning goal and made us champions?

Abby: Yeah, and other reasons. If I get an A in reading, she gets an A plus. If I win the top ribbon for a science fair project, she gets the grand prize ribbon for the whole science fair. If I make first string on a team, she's voted captain. No matter what I do, she does it better.

Class: We're number one! We're number one!

Abby: I'm sick of it! Gina's always number one, and I'm always number two. If I have to shout with everyone, all I can say is *(shouts sarcastically)* Gina's number one! Gina's number one!

Devon: Stop it! Your jealousy is ruining our cheer.

Abby: I'm not jealous.

Devon: Do you wish you were Gina?

Abby: *(Hesitates.)* Some days.

Devon: Do you want to do better than Gina?

Abby: Most days.

Devon: Do you feel like Gina ruins everything you do even when she's nowhere near you?

Abby: Every day.

Devon: That's called jealousy. You think you're not worth anything because someone else has different things they're good at.

Abby: You don't get it at all.

Devon: If Gina does better than you, you feel that everything you do has no value.

Abby: *(Shrugs.)* Maybe.

Devon: You know there's always going to be someone in the world who can do something better than you. Maybe one person will play kickball better, and another will be better at math. If you have to be the best at everything to feel good about yourself, then you will never feel good enough and always wish you were someone else.

Abby: I never thought of it that way.

Devon: King Saul in the Bible had the same problem—he was jealous of David. Saul didn't try to be happy with what he had already done for God, and he wasn't thankful for what God had done for him. Instead, he felt sorry for himself and tried to get rid of David. Maybe you should trust God with your problem, like David did.

Abby: You're right. I shouldn't put myself down because someone does better than me.

Class: We're number one! We're number one!

Devon: It doesn't matter if you're number one or number 37 if you're doing what God wants you to do.

Abby: Then I guess there's only one thing left to say. *(**Devon** and **Abby** smile at each other.)*

Class, Devon, and Abby: We're number one! We're number one! *(They move offstage while still chanting.)*

Curtain Call

■ **Why was Saul jealous of David when he was king and had everything?** *(He was a people pleaser who felt insecure when the people's loyalty seemed to shift to David.)*

■ **What did Abby feel bad about?** *(that Gina had scored the winning goal, that she could never do anything as well as Gina, etc.)*

■ **Have you ever let yourself get down because someone else did better than you? What does this kind of jealousy feel like?** *(Let volunteers briefly share.)*

■ **How can you trust God when you feel jealous?** *(I can thank Him for making me just the way I am, thank Him for the other person and their talents, ask Him to help the other person to use those skills or opportunities to serve Him, etc.)*

Tripped Up

Kids experience that getting even isn't as much fun as trusting God.

Scripture:

1 Samuel 26

Memory Verse:

Hatred stirs up dissension,
but love covers over all wrongs.
Proverbs 10:12

Bible Background

David was running for his life. For years he had to continually look over his shoulder to avoid Saul's murderous intentions. After fleeing from Nob to Gath to a cave at Adullam, all the while relying on others for his food and safety, he ended up in the Desert of Ziph. He had 600 men willing to follow him, but he sacrificed having a home and family in order to follow God's way: He refused to fight the anointed king of Israel.

When Ziphite informers told Saul where David was, David fled to the Desert of Maon, and from there to En Gedi. David had an easy opportunity to kill Saul at En Gedi and rid himself of this relentless pursuer intent on killing him, but David chose to spare Saul.

David returned to the Desert of Ziph, where the Lord caused a deep sleep on Saul's guards, thereby allowing David a second chance to kill Saul. But David knew that God's way was not to kill the king, and he was willing to let God take care of everything. Even when handed the chance to get even, he chose not to.

There are times when it feels someone or some problem is pursuing us, even threatening us. We may become frustrated by a long wait for justice. But like David, we need to resist the urge to take matters into our own hands. We need to turn down opportunities to get even. Can we, like David, trust God in our waiting times?

Summary:

Sandra invites Maria to play with her at recess, but Maria is too busy figuring out how to get even with a boy who tripped her in line. Once Maria realizes that all she's doing is wasting her own time, she learns the same lesson that David did when he had an opportunity to kill Saul: God's way is better than getting even.

Setting: A school playground

Props:

- *(Optional)* **jump-rope or ball for Sandra to carry**

Characters:

- **Sandra**
- **Maria**

Teacher Tip:

Have your characters think through the feelings in this skit and encourage them to work to bring out those feelings in their voices and facial expressions.

Tripped Up

*As the scene opens, **Sandra** walks over to **Maria**, who is sitting on the school playground with arms crossed.*

Sandra: Why aren't you playing foursquare?

Maria: *(Scowls.)* I've got better things to do.

Sandra: Than playing foursquare?

Maria: Some things are more important.

Sandra: Like what? What's better than playing foursquare at recess? You'll lose your title as the foursquare champ if you don't play.

Maria: *(Huffs.)* Drake tripped me.

Sandra: And you hurt your leg and can't move? Why didn't you tell me? I'll get a teacher. *(Turns to go.)*

Maria: I'm fine. It only made me stumble.

Sandra: *(Turns back.)* Did it just happen?

Maria: No. When we were in line to come out for recess, Drake stuck out his foot and made me trip.

Sandra: *(Looks confused.)* I don't get it. Why are you still sitting here?

Maria: I'm going to get even with him.

Sandra: *(Looks surprised.)* Really?

Maria: Of course. I've sat here and thought about it a lot. I'm really close to having a plan.

Sandra: You've done nothing all recess but sit here being mad? *(Rolls eyes.)*

Maria: *(Jumps to her feet.)* You don't understand. If I can figure out how to trip Drake, I'll make sure he won't just stumble—he'll fall hard!

Sandra: And to figure out how to get even with Drake, you're going to waste your whole recess?

Maria: Well, I don't want to use it all up, but I can't just let this go.

Sandra: Why not? Why don't you just forgive him and get on with having fun?

Maria: He ruined my recess.

Sandra: You're sitting here by yourself instead of playing. Who's ruining your recess?

Maria: I don't feel like playing!

Sandra: *(Pulls **Maria** gently to sit down with her. Takes a breath.)* Look, Drake may have tripped you at the start, and that was wrong, but now you're holding on to your mad feelings and ruining your whole recess. You should do this God's way—it's definitely better than getting even. If you forgive Drake, then you can come have fun with us.

Maria: But if I forgive him, I have to forget what he did to me.

Sandra: But then you'll be like David in the Bible. King Saul had been mean to him—really awful. But when David had a chance to hurt Saul back, he didn't do it. Instead, David treated Saul well. And he did it over and over.

Maria: I didn't think about it like that. *(Sighs.)* Getting even sure is hard work, and it's not a lot of fun. *(Pauses.)* Oh, okay. I'd rather act like David than King Saul. I'll forgive Drake for tripping me. Whew. I feel a lot better.

Sandra: *(Stands up.)* Are you ready to play?

Maria: Yeah. *(Stands.)* And I think I might even ask Drake if he wants to play with us.

Sandra: Now that's really forgiving like David!

Maria: But he'd better be careful—I'm the foursquare champion, you know! *(Runs offstage.)* Come on! *(**Sandra** runs after her.)*

Curtain Call

- **Why do you think David was willing to wait instead of killing Saul when he had the chance?** *(He trusted himself to God. He knew God would bring justice. God had told him not to touch the one anointed by God.)*

- **How did Maria feel when Drake tripped her? What did she do?** *(She was mad and wanted to get even. She wasted her recess sitting around thinking of ways to get even.)*

- **What was the example about David from our Bible story that Sandra reminded Maria of?** *(David was hurt and chased and threatened by King Saul, but David decided not to get even when he had the chance; he even showed kindness to Saul.)*

- **When someone's mean to you, what are ways you can turn around the situation instead of getting even?** *(I could forgive by not holding a grudge, by not saying mean things about them, by not getting even, by acting friendly in return, etc.)*

Give Credit

Bragging keeps one talented boy from giving God credit.

Scripture:
1 Samuel 31; 2 Samuel 2:1-7, 11; 5:1—6:19; Psalm 21

Memory Verse:
Ascribe to the LORD the glory due his name. Psalm 29:2

Bible Background

During a battle with the Philistines, three of Saul's sons, including David's best friend Jonathan, were killed. Saul himself was critically wounded and, fearing torture by the enemy, took his own life. Though David was now king, just as the Lord had promised, he mourned the death of Saul.

David settled in the town of Hebron, where the leaders of Judah anointed him publicly as king. For the first 7½ years of his reign, David ruled only over Judah because Ish-Bosheth, Saul's one remaining son, had been proclaimed the king of Israel by Abner, the ex-commander of Saul's army.

Finally, following an argument with Ish-Bosheth, Abner joined David's side and all the tribes declared David as king. With the tribes united, they recaptured Jerusalem from the Canaanite Jebusites and made it Israel's religious and political center.

David never doubted that his strength and the victory were due to the Lord (Ps. 21:1), and he always gave God credit. He recognized that his own strength and knowledge would not make him king or even help him lead his people. He relied on God.

Realizing that we do not have the power to accomplish something can be a wonderful opportunity to rely upon God. His power, strength, and wisdom will never fail. When we are weak, God is strong through us (2 Cor. 12:10). And in areas where we feel strong or talented, we need to remember that every good and perfect gift is from the Lord (Jas. 1:17).

Summary:

When Marcus is able to bat in the winning run, he feels smug in his abilities. But his bragging focuses on himself. Yi Sun challenges him to give God credit for what he can do, since God is the one who created him. Marcus eventually agrees.

Setting: Baseball field

Props:

- Baseball
- Baseball bat
- Baseball cap
- Team shirt
- Two backpacks
- *(Optional)* whistle and a matching team ball cap in adult size

Characters:

- Coach–wearing optional whistle and team ball cap that matches Marcus's
- Marcus–wearing team shirt over his real shirt along with a baseball cap
- Yi Sun
- The team (even just two or three kids)

Teacher Tip:

Encourage your kids to speak their lines slowly and clearly. Remind them that even though it may sound funny to their own ears, an audience can understand slower speech better.

Give Credit

As Scene 1 opens, the team is playing a game, and **Marcus** *swings the bat as* **Coach** *watches from the sidelines. The teammates cheer as if a run has scored. Then they run over and congratulate* **Marcus**. *One of them hands* **Marcus** *the ball, as if he had brought it in from the field.*

Coach: *(Jogs over to* **Marcus** *and pats him on the back.)* Marcus, way to go at hitting that winning run! You are an incredible player. Makes me think of those great players in pro baseball.

Marcus: Wow! Really?

Coach: You're a natural! You're not only on track for a great career, you're great now! You're a brilliant player!

Marcus: *(Smiles big.)* Thank you. I am good, aren't I? *(Raises up arms as if to show off and congratulate himself. The* **team** *looks annoyed. All exit.)*

(Offstage, **Marcus** *removes his team shirt and cap. Then* **Marcus** *and* **Yi Sun** *walk onstage, both wearing backpacks.)*

Marcus: And the coach said I was a brilliant, incredible player.

Yi Sun: You are good at baseball.

Marcus: Brilliant. Coach called me brilliant … and incredible. I'm good, really good. *(Pauses.)* Really, really, really good. *(Stands still, smiling to himself.)*

Yi Sun: *(Stops walking to stare at* **Marcus**.*)* Get real.

Marcus: I'm not just good, I'm amazing.

Yi Sun: Earth to Marcus.

Marcus: I'm probably going to play pro. All due to my exceptional qualities. *(Pretends to carry on a conversation with himself, with a flair.)* Thank you very much, self. You are so welcome. *(Pats himself on the back.)*

Yi Sun: Well, Mr. Brilliant, you know that God gave you your talent.

Marcus: Huh? *(Looks around, almost startled to see someone with him.)* What does God have to do with baseball?

Yi Sun: *(Pretends to think melodramatically.)* Let's see. Hmm. God created you. Therefore, whatever you have that's good was given to you by God.

Marcus: *(Hesitates.)* Well, maybe.

Yi Sun: Not maybe. Think about King David in the Bible.

Marcus: King David liked baseball too?

Yi Sun: I have no idea.

Marcus: I suppose that even if he wasn't a baseball player, David was pretty incredible. He fought lions and bears, killed a giant, led an army, played musical instruments …

Yi Sun: And he loved God. That was most important. When he became king, David thanked God for putting him there.

Marcus: But he was so good at everything.

Yi Sun: Yes, but King David knew it was important to give God credit for the good things that happened in his life.

Marcus: *(Thinks for a moment.)* So, God made me good at baseball. I need to thank Him for what I'm good at.

Yi Sun: Right. What about math?

Marcus: No, just baseball.

Yi Sun: No, I mean, what are you going to do about math? We have that assignment due tomorrow.

Marcus: I forgot all about that. I'm horrible at math.

Yi Sun: Want help, Mr. Brilliant?

Marcus: Yeah. I need all the help I can get.

Yi Sun: As long as you give God credit for the good things, I can show you how to work those problems.

Marcus: I'll give God credit—especially if you show me how to figure out math. *(Exit together.)*

Curtain Call

■ **Who did David give credit to for his victories? Why?** *(He knew that all his strength and every good thing came to him from God.)*

■ **What did Marcus think about his baseball talent?** *(that he was incredible and brilliant—and that it was from his own natural talent and effort)*

■ **What was the example from King David that Marcus needed to follow?** *(David realized that God had made him king, that it wasn't from his own hard work. David thanked God for everything that he was rather than bragging about it.)*

■ **What things are you good at that you can give credit to God for? What wonderful things or experiences do you enjoy that you can thank God for?** *(Let the class name everything they can think of.)*

Taking a Chance with Wisdom

At a carnival game, a boy learns that God gives wisdom when he asks.

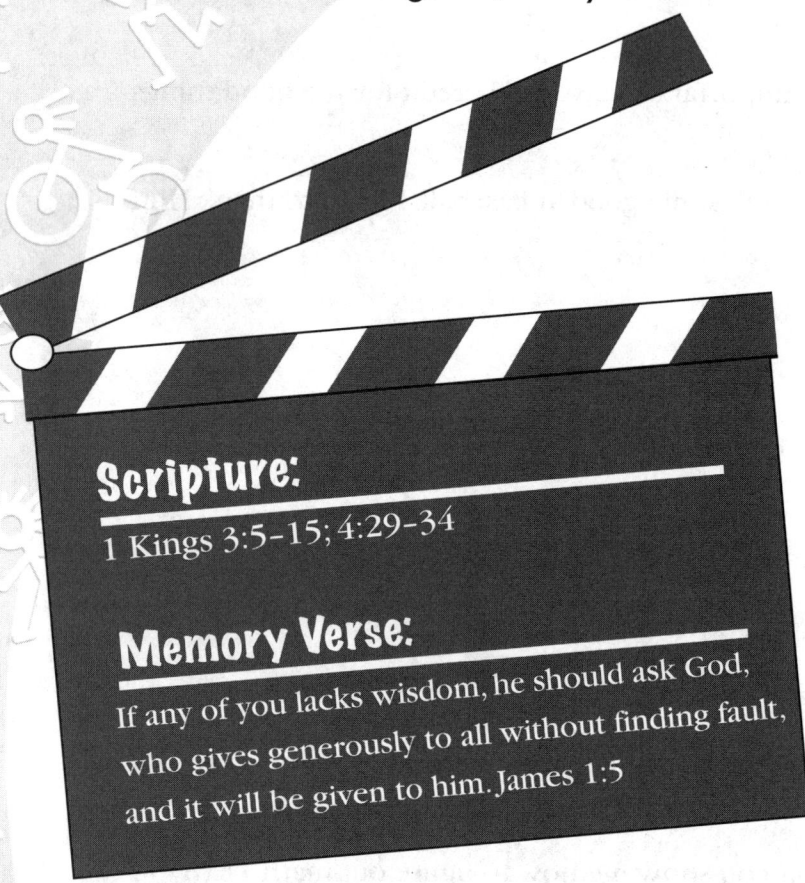

Scripture:

1 Kings 3:5–15; 4:29–34

Memory Verse:

If any of you lacks wisdom, he should ask God, who gives generously to all without finding fault, and it will be given to him. James 1:5

Bible Background

Though Solomon was not David's firstborn son, he was David's chosen heir and so became third king of Israel. Because he was the son of David and Bathsheba, his life was a testimony from God about His willingness to forgive sin. After Solomon's birth, God sent Nathan the prophet to announce God's love for Solomon and to give Solomon a second name—Jedidiah, meaning "loved by the Lord" (2 Sam. 12:24–25).

When God appeared to Solomon in a dream and told him to ask for whatever he wanted, how tempting it may have been to ask for wealth or long life or fame. But Solomon knew how great the task before him was and asked the Lord for wisdom to rule the people well. In response, the Lord not only blessed him with a wise and discerning heart (1 Kings 3:12), but also promised him riches and honor.

Solomon was keenly aware of his inadequacy. He humbled himself before God and admitted his weakness and inability. Solomon's humble and honest attitude is a great example for us when we come to God in prayer. If we come thinking we need only "a little" help or just some guidance in areas where we feel inadequate, we miss an important opportunity to see God in action.

When you pray for wisdom, try to include areas that you already feel confident about, humbling yourself and your human limitations before God. Listen for His guidance in the small details. You'll see His hand in big and small events.

Summary:

Denzel is set on paying money to guess which cup holds the bean at a carnival booth. His first guess is wrong. Kami tells Denzel that a game of chance is wrong and that he should leave this game. Denzel has another idea. He prays for wisdom. In the end, he makes a wise choice and leaves the booth with Kami.

Setting: A carnival booth

Props:

- **Three identical cups**
- **Table**
- *(Optional)* **items to make a carnival booth out of the table—balloons, streamers, stuffed animals, or other prizes**
- *(Optional)* **stereotypical carnival clothing for Tricky Ricky, such as suspenders and a fedora**

Characters:

- **Tricky Ricky**
- **Denzel**
- **Kami**

Teacher Tip:

Set up the table where the audience can clearly see the cup game taking place, and have the actors stand where they won't block the audience's view.

Taking a Chance with Wisdom

*As the scene opens, **Denzel** stands in front of a table where **Tricky Ricky** is moving around three upside-down cups.*

Tricky Ricky: *(In a smarmy con man voice.)* Choose a cup, any cup. No matter what you choose, you won't find the cup covering the bean. My hands are quicker than your eyes.

Denzel: You forget. I watched you put the bean under one of the cups.

Tricky Ricky: Then point it out.

Denzel: I've been watching you since I came to the carnival.

Tricky Ricky: Then take a guess. Your first guess is free. After that, you pay me a quarter each time you guess wrong.

Denzel: No problem. The bean's under that cup. *(**Denzel** points. **Tricky Ricky** lifts the cup, but there is no bean.)*

Tricky Ricky: Sorry, son. *(Continues moving the cups around to confuse **Denzel**. **Kami** walks up to the table.)*

Denzel: How can that be?

Tricky Ricky: The hand is quicker than the eye.

Kami: *(Puts hands on hips and takes a savvy stance.)* Or you cheat.

Tricky Ricky: *(Feigns shock.)* I'm hurt that you would think such a thing. I cannot help it if I'm skilled.

Kami: *(Shakes a finger at him.)* You can help it if your skill is fooling others.

Tricky Ricky: *(Speaks to **Denzel** and waves off **Kami** as if she's an annoying fly.)* She doesn't know what she's talking about. Are you ready to take another guess?

Denzel: *(Hesitates.)* I need wisdom.

Kami: *(Turns to **Denzel**.)* You need more than that. You need a policeman to arrest this sneaky guy.

Denzel: Hey, didn't God say that if I asked for wisdom, He'd give it to me?

Kami: Yeah, but I don't think He meant He'd give you wisdom to win a prize at a carnival booth.

Denzel: I'm going to ask anyway.

Tricky Ricky: Go ahead and ask. Let's see if my hands are quicker than your God's eyes.

Kami: Denzel, don't do it. God isn't a candy machine. You can't just push a button and expect God to give you what you want.

Denzel: I'm not asking for candy. I'm asking for wisdom. (*Bows his head.*) God, please give me wisdom, like you gave King Solomon. (*Lifts his head.*) There, I did it.

Tricky Ricky: (*Laughs.*) You look wiser to me. Are you ready for your second guess?

Kami: Don't do it, Denzel. If you put down a quarter, you'll be betting. God doesn't want you to gamble away the money He's given you.

(**Kami** *grabs* **Denzel's** *arm and tries to pull him away from the carnival booth.* **Tricky Ricky** *grabs the other arm and tries to keep him there. Allow a tug-of-war to continue for several seconds for comedic effect.*)

Denzel: Wait a minute! (**Denzel** *pulls his arms away from* **Kami** *and* **Tricky Ricky** *and steps back.*) I asked God for wisdom, and He gave me wisdom. I don't need either of you pulling on me.

Tricky Ricky: Then step right up and pick a cup.

Kami: God doesn't give gambling wisdom.

Denzel: In this case, He does.

Tricky Ricky: Put down your quarter and tell me which cup the bean is under.

Denzel: God knew I needed wisdom before I even asked for it. So He brought Kami to this booth to warn me. Gambling is wrong, so I'm leaving.

Kami: Now that's godly wisdom. I'll leave with you. (**Kami** *and* **Denzel** *exit.*)

Tricky Ricky: This asking God for wisdom is a dangerous thing. (*Picks up one cup at a time. There is no bean under any of them.*) I can't be tricky when there's a God who can see through cups.

Curtain Call

■ **Why did Solomon's request for wisdom please God so much?** (*because he was humble; he knew he needed help; he knew only God could give what he needed to rule wisely, etc.*)

■ **What did Denzel need wisdom for?** (*to know what to do about the game he was playing, if he should risk his money on gambling, etc.*)

■ **How did Denzel find wisdom?** (*He stopped and prayed after Kami reminded him that he needed wisdom. He trusted that God had sent Kami to stop him from gambling his money.*)

■ **What are some things you could ask God for wisdom about?** (*Let volunteers share.*)

Roll to God

A girl's wild bike ride shows the class that Jesus rolls us into God's arms.

Scripture:

1 Kings 5:1—9:9; Hebrews 9; Matthew 27:51

Memory Verse:

Let us draw near to God with a sincere heart. Hebrews 10:22

Bible Background

Without a tabernacle or any central worship structure, the Israelites entered into the spiritual danger of worship at various high places led by unapproved leaders (1 Kings 3:2), which was forbidden. David further confused the situation by bringing the Ark of the Covenant to Jerusalem and leaving the tabernacle in Gibeon (2 Chron. 1:3-5). When Solomon built a centrally located temple with worship led by Levites, it eliminated the need for high places.

When dedicating the completed temple, Solomon acknowledged that it was not literally God's abode on earth. Not even the heavens could claim to contain God in any sort of physical sense. Through the temple and worship regulations, the Israelites recognized that they had no direct access to the presence of God. Thus the temple and its sacrificial system were an illustration of how the old covenant failed to deal effectively with the sins of humanity. But God made a new covenant through the sacrificial death of Jesus Christ.

Jesus opened the way for our eternal salvation. And that begins now—we can immediately and continually have fellowship with God the Father (Heb. 10:22). Jesus will not force His way into any area of our lives. He waits to be invited in (as in Rev. 3:20). And His life in us is ongoing. Jesus continually serves as a "high priest," interceding for us (Heb. 7:25). So our access to God, as believers, is always open. Will you let your life be an open door to Jesus?

Summary:

A Sunday school teacher asks her class to compare Jesus to things they know or understand. Children act out ways for the others to guess, and they compare Him to a friend, a king, and a good neighbor. Then Cameron pantomimes riding a bike and tells how his little sister stopped pedaling on a hill and let gravity roll her straight to a safe place—their grandmother's arms. Jesus opens the way for us to roll right into God's arms, just as a bike rolls down a hill.

Setting: A Sunday school classroom

Props:
- Chairs

Characters:
- Teacher
- Maddie
- Nadine
- Cameron
- Shawn
- The class (any number of kids)

Teacher Tip:

You might set up the stage to have the chairs near the side facing center, and have the action take place in the clear center spot—where both the audience and the "class" can see. Be sure the actors face front when speaking and doing their pantomimes.

Roll to God

*As the scene opens, the class is seated and the **Teacher** stands at the front of a Sunday school class.*

Teacher: To help us understand Jesus better, let's see if we can think of things to compare Him to—things He might be like to us. But you'll have to act these out for the class to guess.

Maddie: *(Waves hand enthusiastically.)* Can I go first? *(**Teacher** nods. **Maddie** jumps up.)* Nadine, come here. *(**Maddie** links an arm with **Nadine**, and the two skip happily across the classroom.)*

Teacher: Thank you, girls. Does anyone want to make a guess?

Shawn: Well, they look like they like each other, like they're happy to be together.

Maddie: That's right. Jesus is a friend.

Teacher: How is Jesus like one of your friends?

Maddie: He hangs out with me all the time—like Nadine and I do. And when I have something important to say, I can tell Him about it, just like I would tell Nadine.

Shawn: I have one! *(**Teacher** motions him to come forward. **Shawn** steps up.)* Ahem, ahem. *(Dramatically straightens his shoulders, lifts his chin, looks regal; then he pretends to place a crown on his head. He majestically walks from one side of the room to the other, nodding his head to someone occasionally and even giving a royal wave.)*

Cameron: *(Laughing.)* I think you've been taking king lessons.

Nadine: Or watching too many old movies.

Shawn: *(Gives a dramatic royal bow to the class.)* Jesus is like a king. But not the kind that just walks around looking important but not really doing anything.

Teacher: How is Jesus like a king?

Shawn: He's more powerful than anyone. What He says is important, and He's in charge.

Teacher: Good, Shawn. What about you, Nadine? Do you have any ideas?

Nadine: Yes, but mine's hard to act out. *(She gets up and walks to **Cameron**, **Maddie**, and **Shawn**, pausing by each to smile and pretending to give something or chat. Then she returns to her seat.)* See, I told you it was hard.

Cameron: You looked like you went to visit people.

Maddie: And that you took time with each of them—to talk or bring them something.

Teacher: I might call that being a good neighbor, like when Jesus taught that we should love our neighbors.

Nadine: That's right. Jesus helps us and looks out for us. Isn't that what being a good neighbor is?

Cameron: *(Raises his hand.)* Is it my turn now? *(Without waiting for a response, he jogs to the front and pretends to pedal a bike back and forth. The longer he goes, the more amazed the others look.)*

Shawn: Um, are you riding a bike? How can Jesus be like a bike? *(All snicker.)*

Cameron: Easy. I was at my grandma's farm last weekend. My little sister brought her bike because she wanted to learn to ride a two-wheeler. She walked it up the hill behind the barn, sat on it, and started coasting down the hill. But she didn't know how to use the hand brakes yet.

Maddie: Uh-oh. What happened?

Cameron: The bike began to roll faster and faster down the hill toward the barn door—which luckily was open.

Nadine: Did she crash?

Cameron: No. She steered the bike to stay on the path, and it went right into the barn. Grandma saw her coming and grabbed the bike to slow it down, and they tumbled safely into the soft hay.

Maddie: I get it. When your sister coasted—not using her own power—the bike rolled her down the hill toward the barn.

Shawn: So Jesus is like a bike?

Cameron: Yeah. He rolls us right into God's arms.

*(The **class** claps.)*

Curtain Call

■ **Why was it important for the people to have a place to go to worship God?** *(It kept them centered on worshiping God instead of going to high places to worship idols like the nations around them.)*

■ **How was Jesus like a bike in this skit?** *(He carries us straight to God, we don't have to use our own effort to get to God, etc.)*

■ **What would you compare Jesus to, like the kids in this skit?** *(Let volunteers share.)*

■ **In the Old Testament, people could get to God by going to the temple. But when Jesus came, He opened the way to go straight to God. He was like the temple. So what can remind you that Jesus opens your way to God?** *(Encourage each student to choose something—a picture, an object, a symbol—to remind them of this.)*

A Human Machine

Only the one who made the machine knows how it works best.

Scripture:

1 Kings 17:2–16

Memory Verse:

The LORD is good, a refuge in times of trouble. He cares for those who trust in him.

Nahum 1:7

Bible Background

In the account of God's care for Elijah during an extended drought, God chose ironic ways to meet Elijah's needs. First, God provided food for Elijah through ravens. These were considered unclean birds to the Jews because they fed on dead animals. They were also known for their voracious appetites, yet they delivered enough food to meet Elijah's nutritional needs.

Then, after three years of drought, the brook that God had led Elijah to dried up. God then directed the prophet to a Gentile land. This is also ironic since it was the homeland of Jezebel, one of Elijah's enemies, and the heart of Baal worship, yet God provided for Elijah here.

During this time, God used a widow to meet Elijah's needs. Widows were the poorest of people, with no one to support them. The particular widow in this story had nothing left and expected to soon die from starvation. Instead, God fed her, her son, and Elijah, and continued to provide for this woman until the end of the drought.

The help and provision we receive from God is not always what we expect. And sometimes we might even miss a blessing or help because we insist on looking in all the wrong places. God wants us to trust Him for help. Paul understood this when he wrote, "May the God of hope fill you with all joy and peace as you trust in him, so that you may overflow with hope by the power of the Holy Spirit" (Rom. 15:13). What things do you need to trust God with?

Summary:

This skit sets up actors as a human machine. When one part moves, it touches another part, which touches another, and so on, all the way down the line. Kids will see that no matter what they do, right or wrong, it affects others. The human machine will work perfectly only if each person trusts God for the help he or she needs.

Setting: A room

Props:

- Masking tape numbers 1, 2, 3, 4, and 5, placed on the floor in a line with enough room between each so that students' shoulders are touching when standing on the numbers. Be sure that 2 is to the left of 1, 3 is to the left of 2, and so on.
- Five signs labeled 1, 2, 3, 4, 5 to hang on the five actors
- (Optional) microphone to make a powerful offstage voice

Characters:

- Part 1
- Part 2
- Part 3
- Part 4
- Part 5
- Offstage voice

Teacher Tip:

Each Part's movement is done in two distinct steps. Have the Parts practice doing their moves in a slow rhythm before beginning the skit. Remind the actors to be careful as they act this out so they don't bump each other too hard.

A Human Machine

As the scene opens, each part is standing at random on the stage area (not on the numbers), doing its own motion.

Part 1: *Holds both arms out straight in front with hands together, then turns them to the left. The rhythm is arms center, arms left, arms center, arms left. Repeats this motion.*

Part 2: *Stands up straight, then bends over at the waist and reaches left. The rhythm is stand tall, bend over and reach left, stand tall, bend over and reach left. Repeats this motion.*

Part 3: *Holds left leg out to the left side in a gentle kick, then lowers it back down to the floor. The rhythm is kick, feet together, kick, feet together. Repeats this motion.*

Part 4: *Takes one marching step back, then one marching step forward to come back into line; the whole time this part holds out the left arm so that it would be behind anyone standing to the left. The rhythm is step back, step forward, step back, step forward. Repeats this motion.*

Part 5: *Stands still.*

Offstage Voice: Hey, Parts! Are you tired of doing it your own way?

Part 1: I sure am. Nothing happens when I do this.

Offstage Voice: Part 1, do you trust me?

Part 1: Of course. You're the one who made me and taught me what to do.

Offstage Voice: Then move to the number one marked on the floor.

Part 1: Okay. *(Part 1 moves to number one and continues doing its action.)* Um, nothing's happening.

Offstage Voice: It will. Trust me for the help you need.

Part 1: *(Sighs.)* Okay.

Offstage Voice: Is anyone else tired of doing his or her own thing?

Parts 3 and 5: I am.

Offstage Voice: Then Part 3, move to the number three marked on the floor. And Part 5, move to the number five on the floor.

Parts 3 and 5: Okay. *(They move to their numbers and continue doing their actions.)*

Part 1: This isn't working. Nothing's changed; I'll make it better by myself.

(Part 1 moves to number four on the floor. Her actions hit Part 5. Each time she hits him, he should say, "Ow." Part 3's actions hit Part 1. Each time they hit, Part 1 should say, "Stop that." Continue this action long enough for the audience to enjoy the comedic humor.)

Part 2: Don't forget me!

Offstage Voice: I haven't forgotten you. If you move to the space with number two on it, you will be happier.

Part 2: Will do. *(Moves to number two.)* But I feel I'm really more of a number one.

*(**Part 2** moves to the number one space. Everyone sees what the person next to him is doing and moves down one space. Only the number five space is open now. Each time one **Part** touches another **Part**, the **Part** hit should say, "Ow," or "Stop that," or "This doesn't work." Continue in this sequence for several seconds.)*

Part 4: The open space must be mine.

*(**Part 4** moves to space number five. All parts continue moving but nothing happens, except that they hit each other or get stuck on each other and can't move.)*

Offstage Voice: Are you all happy?

All Parts: No!

Offstage Voice: Are you ready to trust my directions?

Part 1: Hmm, well, after all, you did make us.

Offstage Voice: Please move to where I told you, to the number you are.

*(The **Parts** move to their proper spots and continue doing their motions—but not in the same rhythm, so they still hit each other.)*

Offstage Voice: Okay, now listen to me and move on my count. *(Counts slowly.)* One … two … one … two … one … two …

*All the **Parts** do their action in rhythm with the counting. **Part 1** has both arms straight in front. The arms turn to the left on two, then back to the center. **Part 2** bends over just as **Part 1**'s arms turn so that he doesn't get hit. **Part 3** gently kicks the left leg out just as **Part 4** steps back. When **Part 3** turns to the front, **Part 4** steps forward. When **Part 4** steps forward, her arm pats **Part 5** gently on the back.)*

Part 1: Hey, it's working!

Part 2: This is great fun!

Part 3: And it's so much easier.

Part 4: I'm glad we listened to you!

Part 5: We should always trust the one who made us for the help we need.

Offstage Voice: Just as you trust me, the one who created you, people should trust God, their Creator, for the help they need.

Curtain Call

- **Why was it a sacrifice for the widow to feed Elijah?** *(because she only had enough left to feed her and her son one last meal due to the drought)*

- **What problem were the parts having?** *(they weren't doing what they were made to do, they kept trying to do their own thing, their own way, etc.)*

- **How did they finally start working together right?** *(They listened to the one who made them. They trusted the part-maker for the help they needed.)*

- **What kinds of things do you need help with? How do you think God—who made you—could help you?** *(Let volunteers share and suggest ways.)*

Only One

A class science project brings up a discussion of uniqueness—especially God's.

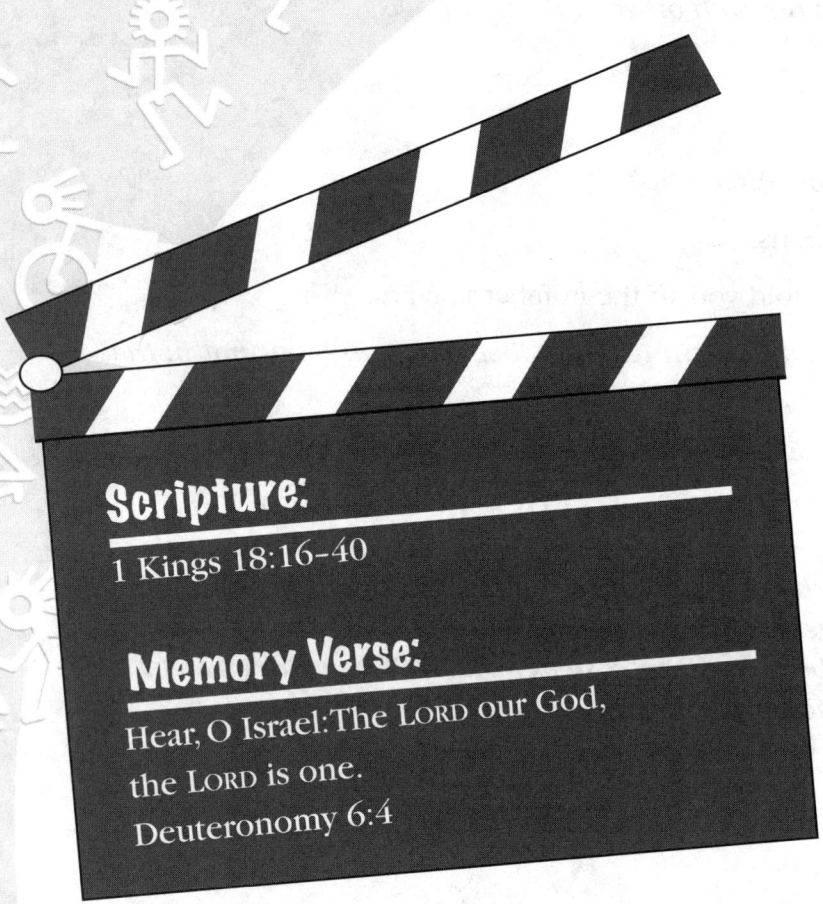

Scripture:

1 Kings 18:16–40

Memory Verse:

Hear, O Israel: The LORD our God,
the LORD is one.
Deuteronomy 6:4

Bible Background

After three years of drought, the people were desperate; yet their leaders refused to turn to God. Instead, King Ahab and his wife, Jezebel, continued to seek the help of pagan gods. God told Elijah to approach King Ahab, whose worship of Baal had angered God earlier. To prove who was the one true God, Elijah challenged Ahab to a contest. The face-off took place on top of Mount Carmel.

Fire was an element of nature that Baal supposedly controlled, so the act of calling down fire from heaven was a direct confrontation to his supposed power. Elijah used 12 stones in his altar to represent the 12 once-unified tribes of Israel. Once God made His sovereignty clear, the drought ended, as did the lives of the false prophets.

The image of God hurling fire upon Elijah's altar is a graphic one. It brings to mind a fierce and jealous God, willing to use terrifying substances to prove He is the only God. Fire symbolizes God's holiness and presence. But that's only one aspect of our God.

God invites us to come closer and trust Him. Isaiah 41:10 says, "So do not fear, for I am with you; do not be dismayed, for I am your God. I will strengthen you and help you; I will uphold you with my righteous right hand." While we draw near to God, we must remember His entire character—from His fearsome power and authority to His gentle, out-reaching love.

Summary:

While working on science in class, Thad, Gabrielle, Carmen, and Alex discover their own uniqueness. Even the twins have different ears, arms, and interests. And they discover that even a litter of puppies has differences. Things in nature are all different, too, like snowflakes and grains of sand. When they recall their Sunday school lesson, they realize that God Himself is unique—there's only one God.

Setting: A school classroom

Props:

- Large pictures (like the kind found in elementary schools) of an ear and an eye
- Large paper snowflake
- Papers and pencils

Characters:

- Twins: Gabrielle and Carmen
- Thad
- Alex

Teacher Tip:

If you don't have twins to play the twin parts, try finding siblings with strong similarities. Otherwise, find two similar looking kids and have them do their hair alike and dress alike.

Only One

*As the scene opens, **Thad**, **Gabrielle**, **Carmen**, and **Alex** are sitting with their school desks pushed together to work on a science assignment. They are looking at large science pictures and fiddling with paper and pencils.*

Carmen: *(Holds up a large picture of an ear.)* I don't think I like seeing our body parts so BIG!

Gabrielle: *(Holds up another picture.)* I like these pictures. It helps me see what we really look like. *(Puts down her picture.)*

Carmen: Do all our ears really look like this? *(Points to her picture.)*

Alex: Your ears and Gabrielle's have to look alike. You're twins.

Gabrielle: Yeah, and we're identical. But even though we look a lot alike, there are little things that make us different.

Thad: Like what?

Carmen: Our ears. My earlobes are connected to my head, and Gabrielle's earlobes aren't.

*(Both **boys** stand up and lean over their desks and stare closely at the **girls'** earlobes.)*

Alex: I never noticed that before.

Thad: Cool. You're right. *(**Both** boys sit back down. **Thad** holds up the picture of the eye.)* But both of your eyes are the same.

Gabrielle: Our eyes are the same, and we like them. *(The two **girls** lean over and put their heads next to each other as if posing for a picture and smile. Then **Gabrielle** leans back up and holds out her arm.)* But look at this. I have freckles on my right arm.

Carmen: But I have freckles on my left arm. *(Holds out her arm.)*

Gabrielle: And I like science.

Carmen: But I don't.

Thad: What does science have to do with anything?

Gabrielle: It shows that even though we look alike, we have differences on the outside and on the inside.

Alex: If identical twins are similar, but not exactly alike, are any two people exactly alike?

Thad: Probably not.

Gabrielle: We all have two eyes, one nose, and one mouth, but we all look different.

Carmen: You're right.

Alex: What about animals? The puppies in our new litter at home sure look just the same.

Gabrielle: Different.

Carmen: And they would have different numbers of hairs.

Thad: And different personalities, no matter how you train them.

Gabrielle: And think about our last unit about weather. *(She holds up the snowflake.)* Remember? If you look at snowflakes under a microscope, you will see that each one has its own unique design.

Alex: How about a grain of sand?

Thad: Different.

Alex: I guess under a microscope they would be different. What about something bigger, like gods?

Thad: There's only one God. That's what the Bible says.

Carmen: And He made each person unique, so each person is special and different in some way.

Alex: But what if there was more than one God?

Gabrielle: Then the world would be a mess. Remember what we learned in Sunday school? The people outside of Israel believed in other gods. They tried to prove which god was strongest.

Alex: Yeah, but Elijah proved to them that their gods were just made of wood and stone— they were fakes. They didn't have any power.

Gabrielle: The one true God proved that.

Thad: It would take one God who loved us very much to create each of us special and different. I'm glad He's the one who made us.

Carmen: Yeah, and besides, the Bible says there's only one God, and that's enough for me.

(All turn back to their papers. Lights out.)

Curtain Call

- **In the Bible story, how did God show that He's the only true God?** *(The god of the other people didn't do a thing. The real God sent down fire from heaven.)*

- **In what ways were the twins alike? How were they different?** *(They had the same eyes, but different ears. They had different freckles and different interests.)*

- **How can knowing the one true God make a difference in your life?** *(Let the kids speculate. They might say that knowing Him brings them salvation, someone to pray to who can help them, etc.)*

The Winning Team

A boy learns no one wins a race on his own when his friends help him.

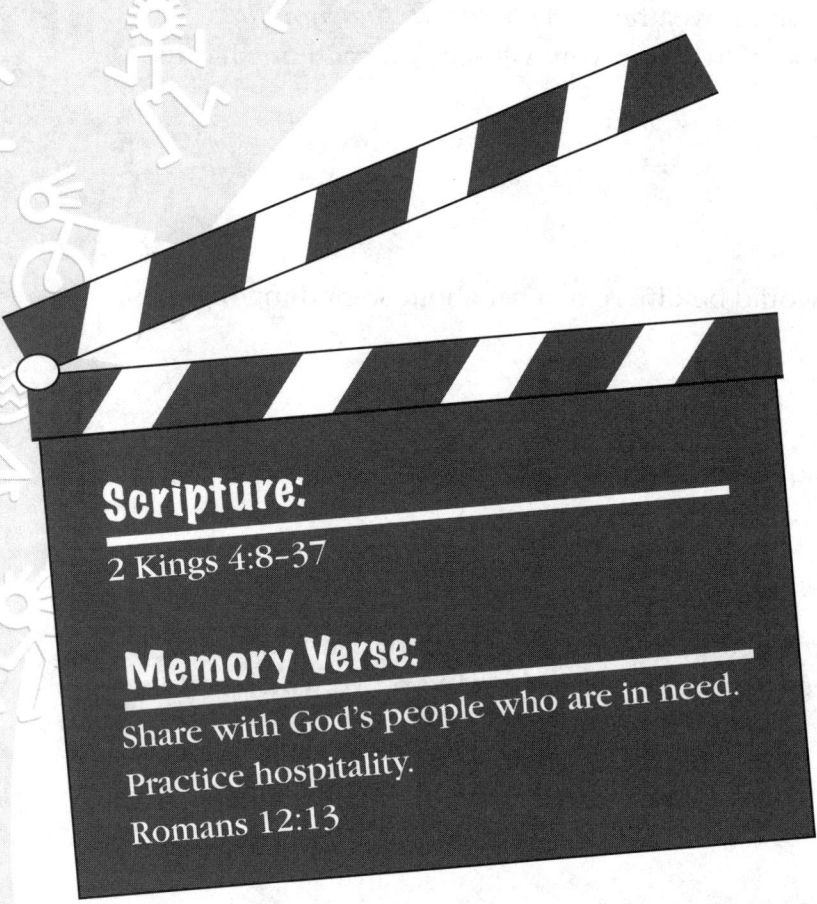

Scripture:

2 Kings 4:8-37

Memory Verse:

Share with God's people who are in need. Practice hospitality.

Romans 12:13

Bible Background

Elisha was the prophet who succeeded Elijah. Elisha delivered the messages from God for over 50 years, through the reigns of six different kings of the northern kingdom of Israel during the ninth century B.C.

The Bible account in 2 Kings 4 took place in the town of Shunem during the reign of King Joram. A wealthy woman living in Shunem recognized Elisha as a man of God, and she began to invite him for meals, as a service to the Lord. Later she and her husband added a guest room so Elisha would have a quiet place to stay when in town.

An elderly, childless woman in a small town in Israel would have limited respect despite her income, yet she offered help in any way she could. Then Elisha, who apparently had access to kings and generals, ended up helping her in a very quiet way—through a prayer for her to have a child. Elisha's simple prayer brought about a miracle, and this couple had their longed-for son.

Jesus knew what He was talking about when He said that it is more blessed to give than to receive (Acts 20:35). Helping others is commanded throughout Scripture, and a vast array of helpful ways is explained and encouraged. What are your spiritual gifts? What are your natural talents? Even without either of these, you could also look for simple opportunities to step up and help someone. Keep a prayerful attitude as you look for ways big and small to help others this week.

Summary:

Ethan and Talia help Rose win a slow-motion race, where the slowest runner wins. Rose is so excited to be the winner that she thinks she did it all herself. Amin reminds her that Ethan and Talia were part of the winning team because they encouraged her and helped her. The kids end up agreeing that those who help others are always winners.

Setting: A race course

Props:
- Masking tape Start and Finish lines at both sides of the stage area
- Chair
- Book
- Three large lollipops

Characters:
- Ethan
- Amin
- Talia
- Rose

Teacher Tip:

If your actors run out of "track," just have them turn around and run back the other way to continue the race.

The Winning Team

*As the scene opens, **Rose** is behind one piece of masking tape, ready to run a race. **Ethan** and **Talia** are nearby. **Amin** is in a different spot onstage.*

Amin: On your marks. Get set. Go!

*(**Rose** runs in slow motion. **Ethan** moves alongside her.)*

Ethan: Come on, Rose, you can do it! Slow it down. Go as slow as you can!

Amin: *(To audience.)* Welcome to the Slow Motion Race of the Year. It's off to a slow start. All the runners are barely moving.

Ethan: Slower, Rose! Come on, you can go slower! *(He continues to move along the race path next to her as he shouts encouragement.)*

Talia: Oh, no! The track may be too clear for Rose.

*(**Talia** hurries forward to put a chair and then a book in **Rose's** way. **Rose** must slowly go around each item.)*

Ethan: You've got it, Rose. You've slowed way down. Keep everything slow!

*(**Talia** hurries in front of **Rose** so she has to turn to go in another direction to get around her.)*

Ethan: Great idea, Talia!

*(**Ethan** also goes in front of **Rose** so she has to turn to go in another direction. They continue doing this until she crosses the masking-tape finish line.)*

Amin: And we have a winner! The last person to cross the finish line is Rose!

Rose: *(Jumping up and down.)* I did it! I did it! I won! I won!

*(**Ethan** and **Talia** congratulate her, then move to the back. **Rose** pumps her arms in the air and jumps around.)*

Amin: *(Walks over to **Rose**.)* Congratulations! Here's your prize—three super lollipops!

Rose: Thank you! I can't wait to eat them—one for lunch, one for dinner, and one for tomorrow. I love winning and doing it all by myself!

Amin: You're not serious are you?

Rose: Of course, I am. I'm going to eat every lollipop all by myself!

Amin: How you divide the lollipops is up to you. What I was wondering is if you really thought you won the race all by yourself.

Rose: Of course I did. Didn't you see me out there? I was the slowest person.

Amin: True, but you had something that the other runners didn't have.

Rose: What do you mean?

Amin: You had someone running alongside you, cheering and helping.

Rose: That was Ethan. *(Points to him.)*

Amin: And you had someone thinking about what was best for you and putting things in your way.

Rose: That was Talia. *(Points to her.)* But you have to admit. *(Points to self.)* I was the one who ran in slow motion and won the race.

Amin: I wonder if you would have been so slow if you hadn't had two friends who were looking for ways to help you.

Rose: I didn't think about that.

Amin: They found ways to slow you down.

Rose: *(Pauses to think.)* When Talia put that chair in my way, it really did slow me down.

Amin: Ethan and Talia helped you, and they knew they would not be the ones to win the race. They did it only for you.

Rose: You know, you're absolutely right. Maybe it's time I tried to think of a way to help them. *(She walks over to **Ethan** and **Talia**.)*

Talia: That was a great run!

Ethan: I don't know anyone who could have done it slower!

Rose: I did run slowly, but thanks to your encouragement and help, I won three super lollipops—one for each of us. *(She hands each a lollipop.)*

Ethan: Thanks, Rose! It's great being a part of a winning team, isn't it?

Rose: Yes—we're a team, and it's great! And when we look for ways to help each other, we are always on the winning team. *(They give each other high-fives.)*

Curtain Call

- **In what way did the woman help Elisha?** *(by giving him meals and later a room in which to stay)* **How did he repay her kindness?** *(He prayed for her to have a son, and God answered that prayer.)*

- **What did Ethan and Talia do to help Rose?** *(They put obstacles in her way to help her win.)*

- **What did Rose have to realize?** *(that her friends looked for ways to help her, that she couldn't have won by herself, etc.)*

- **What are ways you can help kids and adults around you?** *(Help the kids name practical ways, even if small, that they can help others. Kids might suggest sharpening a pencil for a classmate, encouraging a friend to win a race in gym class, helping a friend clean up a mess, etc.)*

When It's Right

When boys do wrong to have fun, they learn that it's not worth hurting others.

Scripture:

2 Kings 5:15–27

Memory Verse:

Better to be poor than a liar.
Proverbs 19:22

Bible Background

A respected Syrian soldier named Naaman traveled to Israel to see the prophet Elisha. Naaman had leprosy, a dreaded disease in that day. Through God's power, Naaman was healed, and he wisely exclaimed, "There is no God in all the world except in Israel" (2 Kings 5:15). This admission was, sadly, more than many Israelites believed. Some Israelites still questioned whether Yahweh (the Lord) alone was God or whether Yahweh and Baal were both gods (1 Kings 18:21).

Elisha's servant Gehazi didn't desire God's glory as the highest reward but rather sought the material gifts that Naaman had offered to Elisha. When he snuck back to ask for money, Naaman reacted to Gehazi with extra generosity and even doubled the amount of money.

Because of Gehazi's wrongdoing, God sent the leprosy of Naaman to cover Gehazi and his descendants (2 Kings 5:27). This is an example of a time when the punishment of the sins of the father continued through the third and fourth generations (Exod. 20:5).

There are times when we are tempted to do something wrong to get what we want. Some sins seem insignificant, like telling a little white lie. After all, who would it hurt for Gehazi to have the money that Naaman had already offered? But sin is always an offense to God. When you desire something you can't have without wrongdoing, call on the Lord's strength and ask Him to conform your desires to what He wants for you.

Summary:

Reed and Chase are bored; they want some fun, something new to do. So they decide to play a mean prank on people. They attach a dollar bill to fishing line and then put the dollar in the middle of the sidewalk while they hide in the bushes, holding the line. When someone reaches to pick up the dollar bill, they yank the string to pull away the money. When the person trying to pick up the money turns out to be their Sunday school teacher, they are reminded of their Bible lesson—that it's not right to do something wrong just to get what they want.

Setting: A sidewalk

Props:

- Dollar bill
- Fishing line attached to the dollar bill
- Bushes (this could be a couple of chairs set together with a blanket draped over them)

Characters:

- Reed
- Stranger #1
- Sunday school teacher

- Chase
- Stranger #2

Teacher Tip:

Since it might be hard for the audience to see how this trick works—it's on the floor and uses clear fishing line—encourage the actors to use overly large actions and exaggerate their movements.

When It's Right

*As the scene opens, **Reed** and **Chase** set a dollar bill attached to fishing line in the middle of the sidewalk. Then they hide behind a bush.*

Reed: This is going to be great!

Chase: Are you sure this is right? It seems awfully mean.

Reed: Nah. How bad can it be? Besides, Chase, weren't you just complaining that you were bored?

Chase: Well, yeah. But it seems like we're doing something wrong.

Reed: Shhh! We have to be quiet or this joke won't work.

*(**Stranger #1** walks across the stage and pauses by the money, then leans over to pick it up. **Reed** yanks the string, and the bill slips away from the stranger's hand.)*

Stranger #1: Hey, what's the big idea? *(Looks around and spies the kids.)* You kids stop playing around here! That's a mean prank!

*(**Stranger #1** shakes his fist at them. **Reed** and **Chase** hide. **Stranger #1** exits. **Reed** and **Chase** peek back out.)*

Chase: That didn't go so well, Reed. That man was really mad.

Reed: I thought it was fun. Besides, do you want to go back to being bored? Don't you want to have some fun?

*(**Chase** nods glumly. **Reed** replaces the dollar bill, and the boys hide behind the bush. **Reed** holds the string, ready to pull it. After a moment, **Stranger #2** enters. She spies the money and bends to pick it up, but **Reed** yanks it away.)*

Stranger #2: Oh my goodness! That was scary. What happened? *(She looks around and spies the boys.)* That's a terrible trick to play on someone! *(She hurries off.)*

Chase: I'm afraid we're going to get caught and get in trouble, Reed.

Reed: Oh, come on. Aren't you having fun?

Chase: Well, kind of. But those people we trick sure aren't!

Reed: One more time, Chase. It can't hurt, can it? *(He replaces the dollar bill, and the boys hide again.)*

*(The **Sunday school teacher** enters, keeping back turned away from the boys so they can't see who it is yet. The **teacher** spies the dollar, bends to pick it up, and **Reed** yanks it a bit.)*

Sunday school teacher: What in the world? *(Looks around and spies the boys.)* Reed! Chase! Why are you hiding in that bush?

*(**Reed** and **Chase** try to stay hidden, looking sheepish. The **teacher** picks up the dollar and slowly follows the string all the way to **Reed's** hand.)*

Sunday school teacher: Hmm, look at this. This must be a new kind of dollar bill they're making—with a string attached. (*Reed* and *Chase* come out but stare at their feet.) Is this yours?

Reed: Um, yeah.

Sunday school teacher: What were you doing?

Reed: It was just a joke. We were yanking the money away when people bent over to pick it up.

Chase: We were only having some fun—because we were bored.

Sunday school teacher: I see. Were the people you fooled having fun with your prank?

Reed: Well, they didn't look too happy.

Chase: They looked mad.

Sunday school teacher: Hmm, yes, I can see that, too. (*Turns over the dollar, thinking.*) Well, since I ended up with this dollar, it looks like I can keep it, can't I?

Reed: (*Looking horrified.*) Oh, but that's my allowance!

Sunday school teacher: (*Pauses to think.*) Do you remember what we talked about in Sunday school last week?

Chase: About not doing what's wrong just to get something we want? I remember.

Reed: And what we wanted was to have some fun. Even if we did something wrong to get it. And now I understand we were doing something wrong.

Sunday school teacher: Boys, having fun isn't wrong at all. You just have to be sure you're not hurting someone else while you're having your fun. (*Looks thoughtfully at the dollar, then hands it to* **Reed**.) Now, can you think of something else you could do with this dollar that would be more fun than this?

Reed: Well, the candy store is having a sale on bubble gum. (*Turns to* **Chase**.) Maybe we could go spend my dollar there. We could have a contest to see who can blow the biggest bubble!

Chase: Yeah! (*They exit.*)

Curtain Call

- **What did the boys in the skit want? What did they do to get it?** (*They were bored and were looking for some fun, but they played a mean practical joke on strangers.*)

- **Even though Gehazi in our Bible story didn't seem to be hurting anyone by asking for the money, why was it wrong?** (*He had to lie to get it, and he tried to fool Elisha into thinking he didn't go and get the money.*)

- **When have you thought about doing something wrong to get what you want?** (*Let volunteers briefly share. The kids might say something like they ignored doing their chores so they could watch TV, or they pushed a younger sibling so they could get first choice of something, etc.*)

Praise Him in Everything

A boy helps a friend with a grumbling attitude to take a second look at his day.

Scripture:

1 Chronicles 29:1-9

Memory Verse:

Come, let us bow down in worship,
let us kneel before the LORD our Maker.
Psalm 95:6

Bible Background

King David had planned that his son Solomon would succeed him on the throne. So David did everything he could to help prepare the future king. One of the big tasks Solomon would face was the building of a temple, and David wanted to make sure everything was ready.

David was thrilled at the people's generous giving to the temple. His response was to praise God for the people's giving, and he led them in worship. David led his people in both preparing for worship and in worship itself.

Preparing for worship in the temple took effort. It took seven years to build the temple. Huge limestone blocks were carved out of rock and hauled miles to the temple site. Cedar was brought in from Lebanon, 100 miles away. Skilled craftsmen worked diligently on the ornate details of this magnificent structure. When the work was completed, the people worshiped with all their hearts, and the glory of the Lord filled the temple (2 Chron. 5:13-14).

It's vital to remember that all we have and are come from the Lord. He deserves the praise for both His gifts to us as well as for our own gifts that we offer back to Him. King David gave his tremendous resources to help build the temple and encouraged people to do likewise. You can give your gifts of praise to the Lord too. Let your life overflow with an attitude of praise to Him.

Summary:

When Matt arrives late for school and misses part of his class's Read 'n' Feed, Kyle finds him in a bad mood. Matt complains about everything going wrong—even things that sound pretty good. Kyle reminds Matt of their Sunday school lesson about praising God, and once Matt tries to look for the good, he also finds reasons to praise God for today.

Setting: A school classroom

Props:

- Two chairs
- Backpack
- Two kids' novels (one inside the backpack)

Characters:

- Kyle
- Matt
- Teacher (offstage)

Teacher Tip:

You might recruit an extra helper to work the lights, so that when the skit is over, there won't be a delay for "lights out" to end the skit.

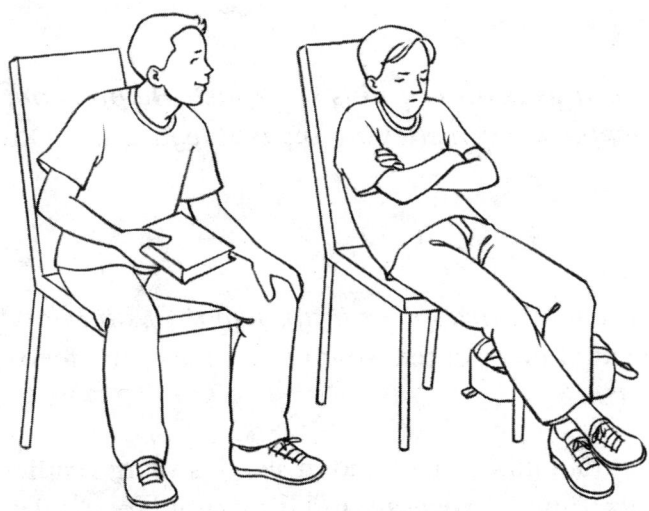

Praise Him in Everything

*As the scene opens, **Kyle** is seated onstage with an empty chair next to him. He's reading a book. **Matt** enters glumly and throws himself down on the chair, dropping his backpack beside him.*

Kyle: What's wrong? Why are you late for school? Our Read 'n' Feed has already started.

Matt: I know, that's bad. And I'm having the worst day of my life too. *(Crosses his arms.)*

Kyle: Bad? But you really like Read 'n' Feed.

Matt: Not today. I'm having the worst day of my life. *(Scowls.)*

Kyle: But you were having such a good day yesterday at Sunday school. Remember? Especially after our class did the activities about praising God. That was a fun lesson.

Matt: That was yesterday. Today is bad. First I spilled my milk at breakfast. I had to change my clothes. Then my mom let me play my new computer game.

Kyle: What's bad about that?

Matt: Because I had to use so much time changing my clothes that I used up most of my free time. So I only got to play for a little while. Then Mom said I had to stop playing and go to school. So I'm mad.

Kyle: But today's Read 'n' Feed. *(Holds up his book.)* We get to just read our favorite books and eat snacks for two hours!

Matt: But it's bad. I was running late because I was mad at my mom for telling me to get off the computer, and I missed my bus. So Mom had to bring me here.

Kyle: But it's great your mom gave you a ride to school. She could have made you walk.

Matt: But now I'm late, so I don't get the whole two hours to read. So it's the worst day of my life.

Kyle: Well, why don't you just get out your book and snack, and maybe your day will get better.

Matt: I doubt it. *(Grumbles as he digs around in his backpack. He pulls out a book, then looks deep into his empty backpack, even sticking his whole face in.)* Oh, no! I can not believe it!

Kyle: What's wrong?

Matt: *(Removes his face from the backpack, picks it up, and drops it heavily on the floor.)* I left my snack sitting on the kitchen counter. Now I don't have the "feed" part of Read 'n' Feed! *(Stands up and kicks his chair.)*

Teacher: *(From offstage.)* Matt, remember that Read 'n' Feed is silent reading. If you don't quiet down, I'm going to have to take time off recess—and it's double recess day.

Matt: See? This really is the worst day of my life.

Kyle: How can double recess be a bad day? I think you need to think again about yesterday's lesson.

Matt: *(Sits down and sighs.)* I give up. What do you mean?

Kyle: I mean, we talked in Sunday school about praising God. And we spent time in cool, creative ways to praise God. But most important, we learned to praise God in all things.

Matt: So?

Kyle: So can't you think of anything good that's happened today that you could praise God for?

Matt: *(Looks at his own book.)* Well, I did get this book I've been wanting from the library. I've been waiting a long time for it to be in.

Kyle: Yeah, that's good.

Matt: And, you're right. It is really good that we get a Read 'n' Feed this morning, even if I missed some of it. And I would have missed even more if Mom hadn't given me a ride.

Kyle: That's right. You could praise God for those things.

Matt: And I'm glad I got to play my computer game a little this morning.

Kyle: And that you had clean clothes ready to change into?

Matt: Yeah, even that. *(In a loud whisper.)* And now that I'm not mad anymore, I'm not being noisy, so I'll still get the double recess.

Kyle: That's the best. *(They give each other a high-five.)* I'll praise God for that one too.

Matt: Yeah, God does deserve our praise. *(Both boys put their heads in their books. Lights out.)*

Curtain Call

■ **What was David's response to the people's generous giving toward building the temple?** *(He led the people in worshiping God.)*

■ **What was Matt doing that gave him a bad day?** *(He was looking at all the things going wrong.)*

■ **How did Kyle help him?** *(Kyle reminded Matt of their Sunday school lesson about praising God and helped him think about all the things going right that day.)*

■ **What are some things you could praise God for that have happened to you today?** *(Let volunteers share.)*

Surprise!

Waiting for a surprise party is hard—like waiting for God's answers to prayer.

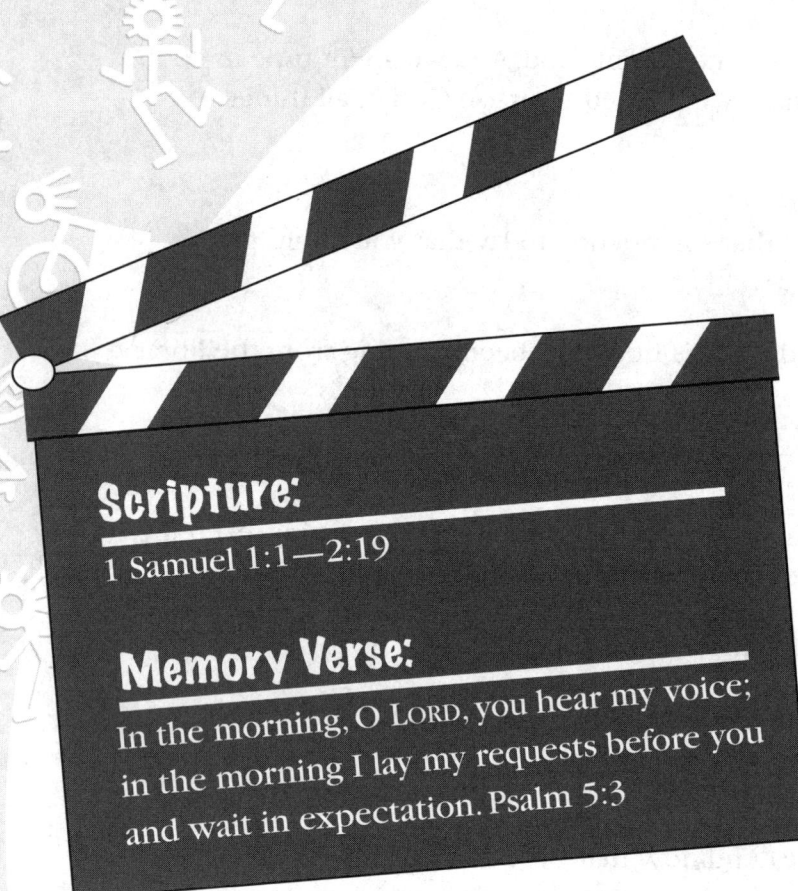

Scripture:

1 Samuel 1:1—2:19

Memory Verse:

In the morning, O LORD, you hear my voice; in the morning I lay my requests before you and wait in expectation. Psalm 5:3

Bible Background

Hannah was a godly woman married to a God-fearing man from Ramah. She was one of two wives of Elkanah, and three times a year they made a pilgrimage to Shiloh. Shiloh was Israel's religious center and the place where Hannah encountered the priest, Eli, during one of these pilgrimages. Both Ramah and Shiloh are a short distance north of Jerusalem.

Eli was a devout servant of the Lord, and he was serving in the place of worship when Hannah was there praying. Not being able to have children brought Hannah humiliation and a sense of failure. Children were vital to the continuation of the family, both in lineage and in providing for the aging parents.

God spoke through Eli to Hannah. When God finally granted Hannah's long-standing prayer for a child, she in turn thanked God by dedicating her son to God's service. Parents of that era could offer their unborn offspring to God as a Nazarite vow.

In 1 Samuel 2:1-10, we see Hannah's attitude about waiting on God to answer a prayer: "There is no one holy like the LORD; there is no one besides you; there is no Rock like our God . . . The LORD is a God who knows . . . He will guard the feet of his saints . . . It is not by strength that one prevails." Think about a prayer you've been waiting for an answer to. Try praying Hannah's prayer of praise about this very thing as you wait.

Summary:

Tate, Daya, Armand, and Alexandra are planning a surprise party for their teacher, Mrs. Williams. But the waiting is driving Daya crazy. Her friends keep her from accidentally spilling the secret, and they remind her of what they learned in Sunday school—that sometimes we have to wait on God to answer our prayers.

Setting: A classroom

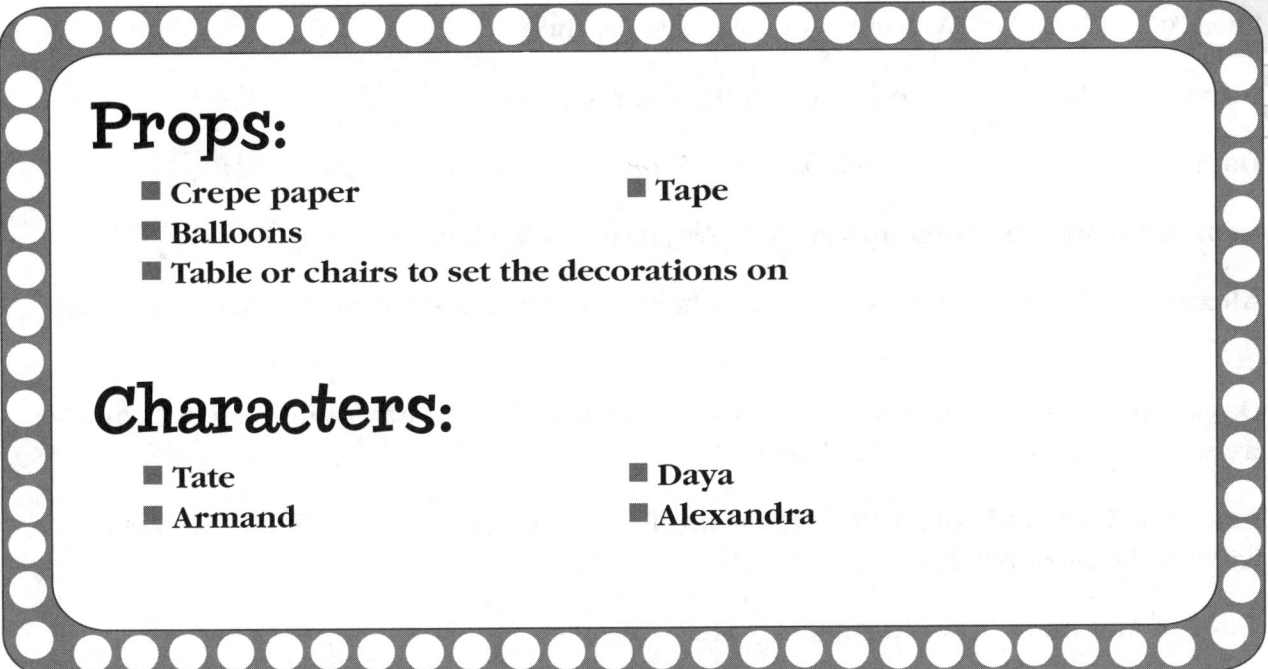

Props:

- Crepe paper
- Balloons
- Table or chairs to set the decorations on
- Tape

Characters:

- Tate
- Armand
- Daya
- Alexandra

Teacher Tip:

If your actors need to hold a copy of their scripts, try putting each on a clipboard—it's easier to keep it from flopping over and can sometimes be disguised as a prop.

Surprise!

*As the scene opens, **Tate**, **Daya**, and **Armand** are decorating the classroom with crepe paper and balloons.*

Daya: I can't wait any longer! When is Mrs. Williams going to come? *(She heads for an imaginary door off to one side. **Tate** grabs her arm and pulls her back.)*

Tate: We don't want her to come yet! We're not ready.

Alexandra: *(Hurries into the classroom through the same imaginary door.)* I managed to delay her really well. She won't be here for at least 10 more minutes.

Tate: Where was Mrs. Williams when you last saw her?

Alexandra: She was in the office, talking to the secretary.

Daya: Maybe I should go check on her. *(Heads for the door.)*

Armand, Tate, and Alexandra: NO! *(**Daya** comes back to the group.)*

Alexandra: Daya, we all know you can't keep a secret. And we want Mrs. Williams to be surprised.

Daya: But surprise parties are so fun. And it's so hard to wait! Can't I just go check and see where she is now? *(Heads for the door.)*

Armand, Tate, and Alexandra: *(In unison.)* NO! *(**Daya** comes back and continues to fiddle with the decorations.)*

Tate: So Alexandra, how did you delay Mrs. Williams?

Alexandra: Well, first I told her to check in at the office. The secretary is in on our secret, and she promised to keep talking to Mrs. Williams for as long as possible.

Armand: That's great. But what if the secretary gets a phone call or something?

Daya: Maybe I ought to go check and see … *(Heads for the door.)*

Armand, Tate, and Alexandra: *(In unison.)* NO! *(**Daya** comes back.)*

Armand: *(To **Alexandra**.)* What's your backup plan?

Alexandra: Well, I also told Mrs. Williams that Mr. Anderson was having a hard time with trying to carry the volleyball nets in from outside and would need some help and so if she had time, she should go out and see if he still needed her. And he had already agreed to me that he would help stall her too.

Daya: I could just run outside and see if she's there … *(Heads for the door.)*

Armand, Tate, and Alexandra: *(In unison.)* NO! *(**Daya** comes back.)*

Tate: But what if Mr. Anderson's done when Mrs. Williams gets finished in the office?

Alexandra: Well, then, I already asked Mrs. Williams's permission for a few of us to stay after school and straighten up the classroom, and I even told her we wanted to make it look really good as a surprise for her.

Daya: You told her about the surprise?

Alexandra: No! Just that we're cleaning up the classroom. She said that'd be fine and that she wouldn't hurry back.

Daya: I could just peek out of the classroom and see if she's coming … *(Heads for the door.)*

Armand, Tate, and Alexandra: *(In unison.)* NO!

Daya: *(Stamps her foot.)* But waiting is so hard!

Armand: It sure is, Daya. But do you remember what we talked about in Sunday school the other day?

Daya: That sometimes we have to wait for good things?

Tate: Exactly. We learned in the Bible that God doesn't always answer our prayers right away. And sometimes the good things He's promised take awhile to get to us.

Armand: But we can always count on God to come through in the end. Waiting for Mrs. Williams to get here for her surprise party is like waiting for God's answers to our prayers.

Daya: I'm not very patient waiting for God to answer my prayers either … But if that's what I have to do, I'll just try to have fun while we wait. *(Grabs a balloon to blow up.)*

Tate: *(Points to an imaginary clock on the wall.)* Hey! Look how late it is! I bet she'll come soon. *(Looks at **Daya**.)* Do you just want to peek out the door?

Daya: *(Runs to the door, pretends to open it a crack and peek out; then she closes it and turns around.)* She's coming!

*(The **kids** hide behind the table or chairs. After a moment, they jump up and yell, "Surprise!" Then lights out.)*

Curtain Call

■ **What was hard for Daya to wait for?** *(for Mrs. Williams to show up for her surprise party)*

■ **What did the woman in our Bible story have to wait for?** *(for God to answer a prayer about having a baby)*

■ **What kinds of prayers have you seen God answer right away? What have you had to wait for His answer on?** *(Allow volunteers to share.)*

Love God

Charades and kids' ingenuity help the class think of ways to love God.

Scripture:

Daniel 6

Memory Verse:

Teach me, O Lord, to follow your decrees; then I will keep them to the end.
Psalm 119:33

Bible Background

Daniel had come to Babylon as a very young man and had demonstrated such integrity that he climbed the ranks of the foreign government. King Darius had appointed him to be one of the three chief administrators over the kingdom's 120 provinces and their satraps, or governors.

King Darius had taken over the rule from Belshazzar the Babylonian at age 62 (Dan. 5:31). It is interesting that historical documents do not mention a Persian king at this time by the name of Darius. This does not discount Darius as a real person. He could have had a role as governor appointed by Cyrus, or possibly Darius the Mede was the name Cyrus used in Babylon.

The lions' den in today's story was most likely an enclosure with room for a spectators' gallery around the open top. There might have been a small entrance off the side, which is where Darius would have set his seal.

In Daniel 6 we find Daniel proving his love for God by spending time in prayer every day, no matter what. He was completely devoted to God, and this was public knowledge. And his devotion to God caused his behavior to be unimpeachable. When we love God, our time spent with Him moves from burden to joyful relief. When we love God, we are changed from the inside out. Loving Him every day in every way will help us become more like Christ, our ultimate goal (Rom. 8:29).

Summary:

The teacher helps the whole class act out how and when and where they can love God—some ways are humorous and some are serious.

Setting: None

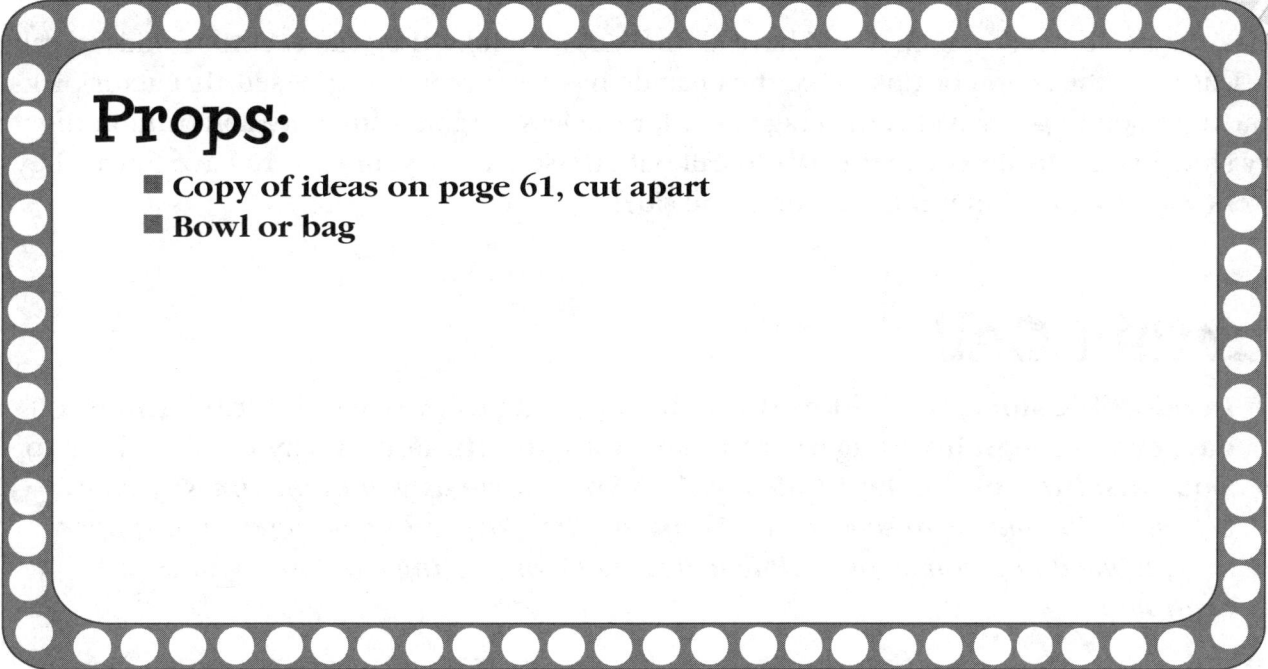

Props:

- Copy of ideas on page 61, cut apart
- Bowl or bag

Teacher Tip:

This is a great chance to let the less dramatic kids in your class have a chance to try their hand at acting. Encourage them to have fun with this drama activity as they work at being uninhibited!

Love God

Photocopy the list on the following page, and cut apart the ideas. Feel free to change any to suit your class. Fold each slip in half once, and place them all in a bowl or bag.

Today we'll play a game of charades showing how, where, and when you can show love to God. Each of us will take turns pulling a slip of paper out of the bowl and then acting out what's written on the paper for the rest of us to guess. You can use any motions or actions, and you can even make sounds, using your voice or things in the room for sound effects, but you can't use any actual words.

Ask for a volunteer to go first, and have all the kids sit where they can see. Allow kids to call out ideas once the action begins. Once the charade has been correctly guessed, that actor picks the next person to go. Provide encouragement for the less-outgoing students, and caution the lively students not to always be the first to call out guesses. Allow your class to have fun as they express ways to love God using their dramatic side!

Curtain Call

■ **In our Bible story, Daniel loved God by stopping to pray to him three times a day, even though it was against the law. Can you think of a way to show love to God each hour of the day?** *(Allow kids to brainstorm as you name times of day: getting up, breakfast, at school, lunchtime, on the playground, doing chores, suppertime, while doing homework, while watching TV or playing computer games, at bedtime.)*

■ **What are other ways you can show love to God? Where are places you can love Him?** *(Let volunteers share more ideas.)*

■ **If you could make a reminder to help you remember to love God at times that you usually don't think about Him, what would it be?** *(Help the kids brainstorm simple ideas, such as wearing a clip watch or wristwatch when they normally wouldn't, drawing a picture or word on the back of their hand with a washable marker, wearing a sticker, hanging a sign on their mirror, etc.)*

Reading the Bible	Praying	Singing
Flying	Swinging	Sleeping
Eating	Doing schoolwork	Riding in a car
Feeding a pet	Dancing	Building
Painting	Playing catch	Running
Swimming	Shooting hoops	Jumping rope

Follow the Leaders

Dressing up like a godly leader doesn't make a boy godly the way he wishes.

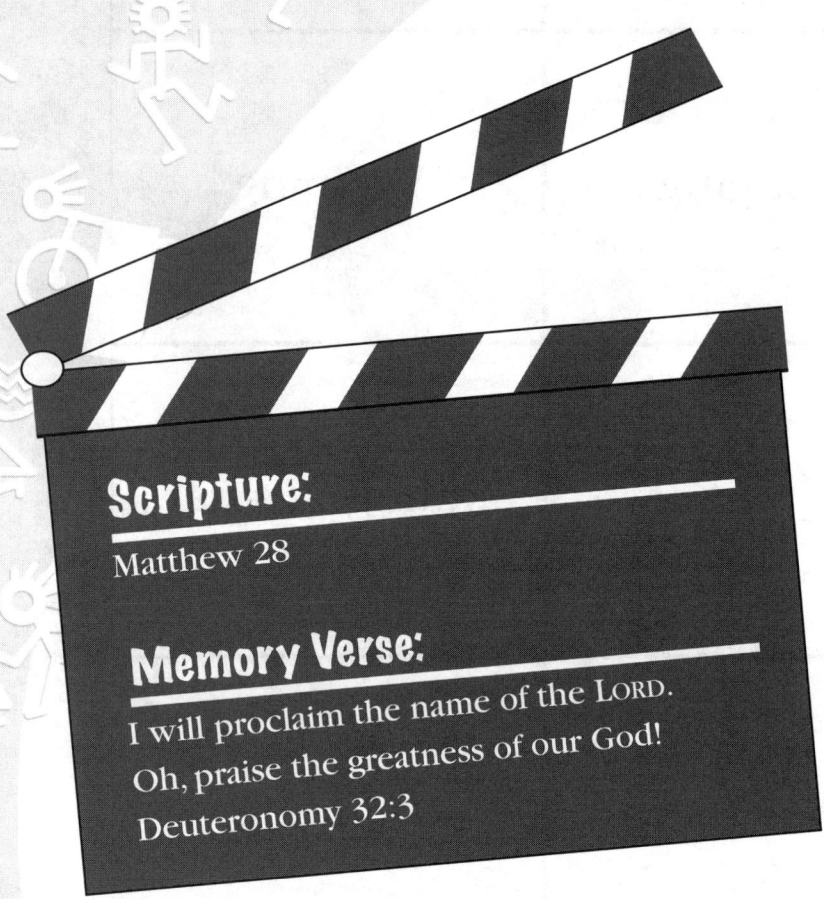

Scripture:

Matthew 28

Memory Verse:

I will proclaim the name of the LORD.
Oh, praise the greatness of our God!
Deuteronomy 32:3

Bible Background

In Jesus' day, women could not be called as legal witnesses in a Jewish trial because their testimony was not considered reliable. Yet God entrusted them with the greatest message of history—that Jesus had risen from the dead! And these were the people from whom the rest of the disciples—all men—were compelled to learn.

Both of the women in today's story had followed Jesus and served Him. Both had watched Him die (Matt. 27:55-56). Both had watched as Jesus' lifeless body was placed in the tomb that was sealed with a large stone (Matt. 27:59-61).

On the Sunday after Jesus' crucifixion, Mary Magdalene and "the other Mary" (perhaps the one in Matt. 27:56) went to Jesus' tomb. This grave was a cave dug into stone cliffs and was borrowed from Joseph of Arimathea, a man of means (Matt. 27:57).

Sometimes the people we should learn about God from are not the first ones we might choose. They might not be the personalities we are immediately drawn to, or their appearance may not impress us. As with the women in the Bible story, God can use anyone to spread His message.

Are you willing to learn from the teachers and leaders the Lord has placed in your life? And are you willing to be used by Him in situations where you don't naturally feel comfortable? Open your heart to the Christians around you, and let yourself teach and be taught by others who follow God.

Summary:

Patrick wants to follow God like the Christians in his life. His friend Neesha decides to help him. So Patrick puts on a jacket to be like the pastor and a hat to be like his grandfather. He carries a baton like the worship leader, some Bibles like the youth pastor, a cane like his grandmother, and a large bag of snacks like his mother. When he tries to lift a stack of paper plates to be like the Sunday school teacher, he realizes that the load he's carrying is too heavy. His mom explains that he doesn't need to look like each godly person but rather to act like him or her.

Setting: A Sunday school classroom

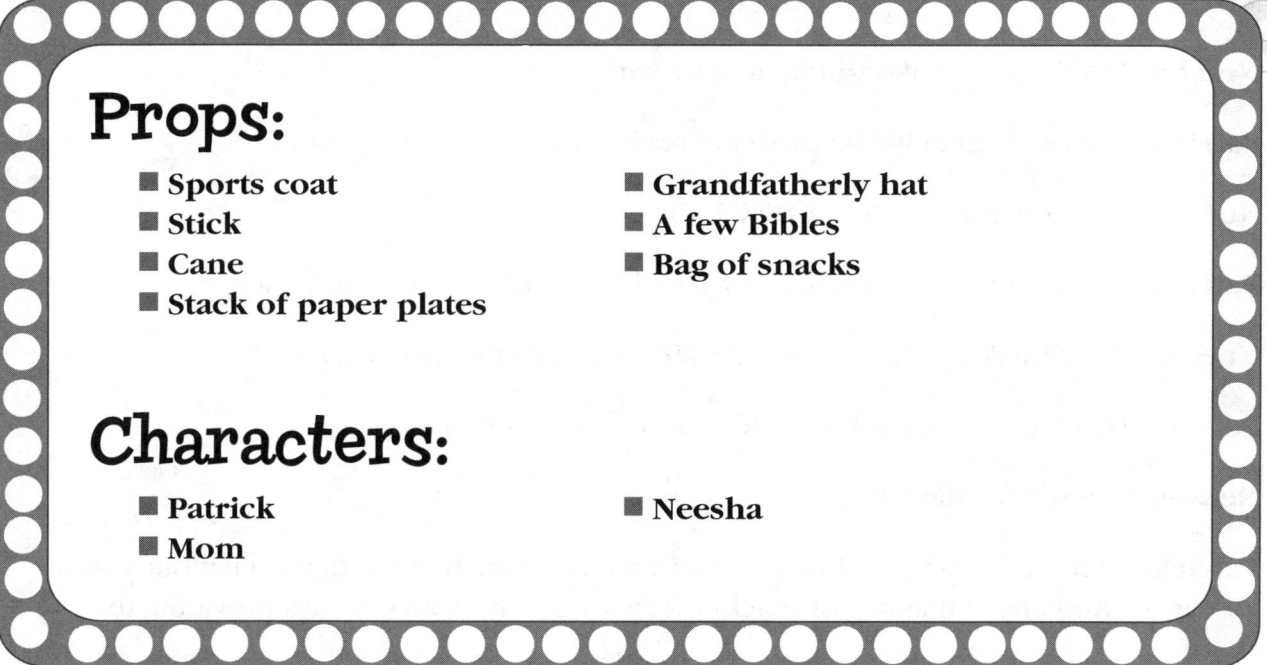

Props:

- Sports coat
- Stick
- Cane
- Stack of paper plates
- Grandfatherly hat
- A few Bibles
- Bag of snacks

Characters:

- Patrick
- Mom
- Neesha

Teacher Tip:

Remind your actors to always face the audience, or to at least direct their voices to the audience, even when facing to the side or moving around the stage area.

Follow the Leaders

As the scene opens, **Patrick** *and* **Neesha** *stand next to the pile of props.*

Patrick: Here's everything I need.

Neesha: It's cool that you're going to learn from people who follow God. Put on the jacket first.

Patrick: Okay. *(Puts on a jacket.)*

Neesha: It looks just like Pastor Everett's.

Patrick: Good. Because I want to look like him. What do you think about this hat? *(Puts on a hat.)*

Neesha: That looks just like your grandpa's hat.

Patrick: It does. My grandpa follows God really well, just like our pastor.

Neesha: What's this? *(Hands the stick.)*

Patrick: I couldn't find a baton like our worship leader, so I'm using a stick.

Neesha: Good thinking. Here's the cane. *(Hands* **Patrick** *the cane.)*

Patrick: That will help me follow God like my grandmother.

Neesha: Can you handle more?

Patrick: I have to, if I want to follow God. Hand me those Bibles—that's what our youth pastor carries. And I need that bag of snacks too, because my mom's always providing the snack.

Neesha: Here you go. *(Hands* **Patrick** *the Bibles and a bag of snacks.)* They're heavy. Are you sure you want them?

*(***Mom*** *quietly enters and watches.)*

Patrick: Of course. God wants me to follow Him. One of the ways I can do that is by looking like the people I know who follow God. What's next?

Neesha: There's only one more thing. *(Hands* **Patrick** *a large stack of paper plates.)*

Patrick: I've got it. *(He tries to walk.)* I've got it. *(Things start to fall.)* Oh, no! I haven't got it. *(He drops everything.)*

Mom: What are you kids doing?

Neesha: I'm helping Patrick learn from people who follow God.

Mom: But what are all these things for?

Patrick: Well, I tried to wear a jacket like our pastor's and a hat like grandpa's. And I tried to hold a cane like Grandma, a bag of Bibles like my youth pastor, and a bag of snacks like you. And when I tried to hold the paper plates, like my Sunday school teacher, it was too much. I'll never be able to follow God.

Mom: Did you know that learning from people who follow God doesn't mean that you have to dress like them or carry around the things they use?

Patrick: Really?

Mom: Really. You learn from what they do, not from how they look.

Neesha: Really?

Mom: Really. Think about this: How do your grandparents show God's love?

Patrick: They look for ways to help people.

Mom: So, if you want to be like them, look for ways to help people.

Neesha: I see.

Patrick: I don't.

Mom: What are ways the worship leader, our pastor, your Sunday school teacher, and your youth pastor follow God?

Patrick: Well, for one thing, they tell everybody about Jesus.

Mom: Right. So to learn from them, tell others about Jesus.

Neesha: I get it. I think I'll be like our church janitor and help Patrick pick up this mess.

Patrick: Really?

Neesha: *(Laughing.)* Really!

Curtain Call

■ **Who did God use to tell the disciples that Jesus was alive?** *(the two women)* **Why was this important?** *(because women were not well thought of at that time, but God used them to spread this important message)*

■ **What did the adults named in this skit do to follow God?** *(looked for ways to help others, told others about Jesus, helped pick up, etc.)*

■ **Who are people you know who follow God?** *(Let volunteers name people.)*

■ **What do these people do to follow God, and what could you do that's similar?** *(Help kids think this through and apply it.)*

Whose Birthday Is It?

Generic birthday parties are no fun—and neither is Jesus' birthday without Christ.

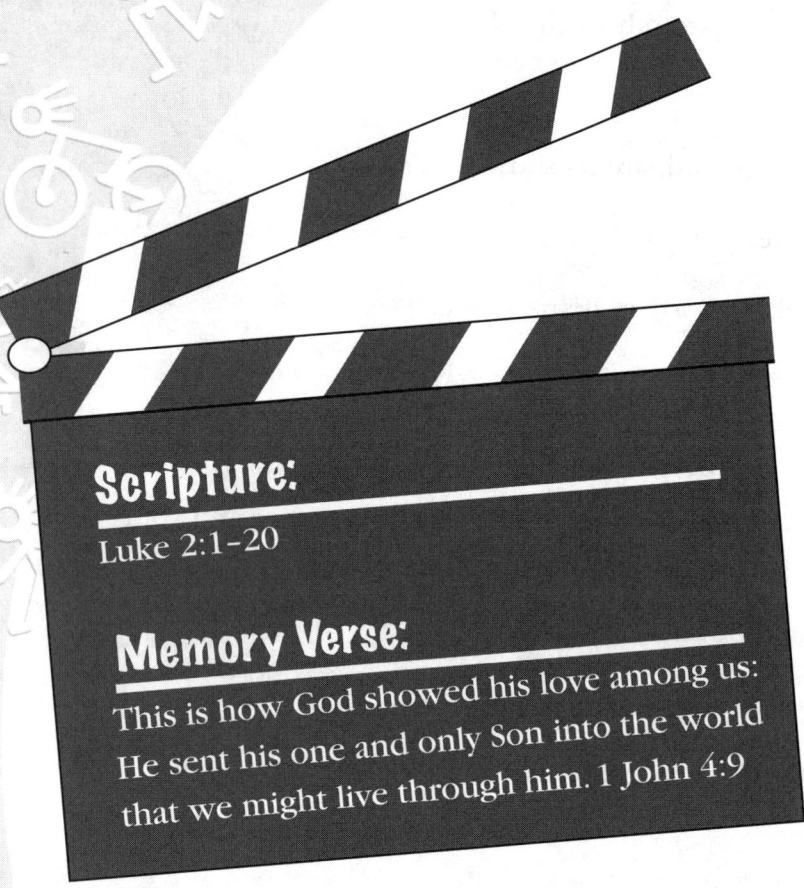

Scripture:

Luke 2:1–20

Memory Verse:

This is how God showed his love among us: He sent his one and only Son into the world that we might live through him. 1 John 4:9

Bible Background

In many Middle Eastern cultures in Bible times, shepherds usually occupied a very low social position. Some shepherds owned the sheep they tended, but most did not. And they usually spent day and night with their sheep, often spending long weeks away from their families as they constantly led their sheep to green pastures. Under such isolated and nomadic conditions, many of the hired men tended to become coarse and hardened.

Since shepherding was a difficult and unpleasant job, applicants were often poor and desperate men. Over the years, shepherds developed a reputation for raiding the villages near the pastures where they grazed their sheep. The fact that God announced the Savior's birth to shepherds is both surprising and reassuring. Jesus came to be the Savior for everyone.

When the shepherds near Bethlehem were surprised by the angels, they were not totally unfamiliar with what was being announced. The shepherds, like all of God's people, were longing for the Messiah. So it is no wonder that the shepherds eagerly responded to the great news of Jesus' birth.

The shepherds' response in Luke 2:8–20 was personal. Focusing on Jesus led them to kneel and worship. They recognized something in the angels' announcement and the presence of this baby that made them realize the deity before them—for Jewish men would never worship a mere human. Then they committed themselves to telling everyone that Jesus their Savior was born.

How can you make your response to Jesus more personal? How can you better worship Him for being God in the flesh?

Summary:

A teacher helps her class see that Jesus' birth is the reason for celebrating by demonstrating with a child's birthday. She takes away the child's name, presents, and cake. When the child complains that the celebration really isn't his birthday party, she compares it to how Jesus must feel when the world takes Him completely out of our celebration for His birthday.

Setting: A Sunday school classroom

Props:

- Large cardboard box for a sheet cake (can be empty, since the audience won't actually see it)
- Bag of carrots
- A well-used "Happy Birthday" sign
- Package of birthday candles
- Cake server or spatula
- Tape
- Ice cream scoop
- Table
- Grocery sack

Characters:

- Teacher
- Brianna
- Noah
- Class (a few kids)

Teacher Tip:

Encourage your actors to think of natural ways to move around the stage to express their roles.

Whose Birthday Is It?

*As the scene opens, the class is seated, with **Brianna** and **Noah** near the front. The **teacher** enters holding the cake box and a grocery sack containing the other props. She sets all these on the table.*

Brianna: Oooh, what's going on today? What's in the box? *(Comes to the table to look at the cake.)*

Teacher: Today we're going to celebrate Noah's birthday. I brought some special things to celebrate this special day. *(Removes the package of candles, the ice cream scoop, and the cake server from the sack and sets them on the table.)*

Noah: Wow, thanks! My birthday usually gets lost in all the holiday stuff this time of year. *(Comes to join **Brianna** and the **teacher** at the front.)*

Teacher: That's just my point: "Holiday stuff." We'll learn something about that too.

Brianna: When do we get to eat?

Teacher: First we have to do a few things. *(She tapes the beat-up "Happy Birthday" sign to a wall or the front of the table.)* This sign gets used for so many people. One birthday's just like another. *(**Brianna** and **Noah** look at each other.)*

Brianna: But this is just for Noah's birthday. Couldn't we make a sign that says "Happy Birthday, Noah"?

Noah: It would mean more.

Teacher: Sorry—no time, no room. But you know it's for you, don't you?

Noah: Um, sure. That's okay.

Brianna: But to make up for the sign, let's put lots of candles on the cake.

Noah: I can hardly wait!

Teacher: I'm afraid the candles are a fire hazard, so we won't be able to use them. *(Dramatically drops the candles back in the sack.)*

Noah: What about the cake? We can still eat it, can't we?

Teacher: Well now, I'm not so sure, now that I think about it. The sugar in cake can cause children to become more energetic than usual. You all will be bouncing off the walls. *(Dramatically drops the cake server back in the bag.)* How about we do something healthy instead? We can have carrots. *(She takes the bag of carrots from the grocery sack and sets it on the table with a flourish. Then she moves the cake box out of the way. **Noah** and **Brianna** look more disappointed.)*

Brianna: Carrots? That's not much of a birthday tradition. What about ice cream?

Teacher: Some of the kids are lactose intolerant. That means that they can't eat milk products. *(She drops the ice cream scoop back in the bag.)*

Brianna: But do you think we could at least give some birthday presents to Noah?

Noah: Definitely!

Teacher: I'm afraid we can't do that either. If Noah gets a present, every child will want one. And since we don't want anyone to feel left out, we won't sing "Happy Birthday" either. In fact, maybe we shouldn't even say his name—wouldn't want anyone's feelings to be hurt!

Noah: Wait a minute! I get a beat-up sign and some carrots? What kind of birthday party is that? You're not even going to say my name. No one will know it's my birthday.

Teacher: True, but I thought you'd be okay with the changes. After all, it's what we often do at the time of Jesus' birth. We forget whose birthday it is.

Noah: What do you mean?

Teacher: Some people won't focus on Jesus because they don't want to offend people who don't believe in Jesus.

Noah: Oh, I get it. You can walk through so many stores this time of year and not even know what the celebration's about. Everything's red, green, and glittery, but no one says why.

Brianna: On Jesus' birthday, we need to celebrate Jesus' birth, just like on Noah's birthday, we should celebrate Noah's birth.

Teacher: That's right. Because leaving Jesus out of His birthday is like leaving Noah out of his birthday!

Brianna: I'll be sure to remember that.

Teacher: And now let's really have a birthday party—for Noah. *(Brings cake box back to the center.)*

Noah: And for Jesus!

*(All the **kids** gather round. Lights out.)*

Curtain Call

- **In the skit, how was Noah's birthday made less special?** *(by not having his name on the sign, by not singing him the birthday song, by not doing certain special things because the teacher was afraid of offending someone, etc.)*

- **What are ways we can celebrate and remember that it's Jesus' birthday?** *(by putting up decorations that remind us of Him, by singing carols rather than generic seasonal songs, by telling everyone why we celebrate, etc.)*

- **What are things your family or our church does to celebrate Jesus' birthday?** *(Let volunteers name things.)*

Our Family

A family ride in the minivan helps two kids think through what caring is all about.

Scripture:
John 11:1–44

Memory Verse:
Love one another. As I have loved you, so you must love one another.
John 13:34

Bible Background

Only John's gospel describes the events surrounding the death and resurrection of Lazarus. Jesus had been preaching in villages west of the Jordan River when news came of Lazarus's illness. Lazarus was in Bethany, probably 30 or 40 miles from where Jesus was.

The raising of Lazarus caused another uproar among the Jewish leaders and caused more Jews to follow Christ; so much so that the religious leaders considered executing Lazarus as well as Jesus (John 12:1–11).

Mary and Martha were deeply grieving the death of their brother, Lazarus. They knew their friend Jesus could help. But they were unprepared for the depth of Jesus' own grief and the miraculous way He met them in their time of family need. They had deep faith in Jesus, but Jesus wanted to develop their faith even deeper and bring glory to the Father. So He allowed them to go through a very trying time.

You have probably been through hardships that have tested your faith. When our trials concern our most-loved family members, our faith is most tested. As much as we love our families, we must trust that He loves them even more. And as much as we love Jesus, we must allow Him to stretch and deepen that love, trusting Him even unto death. Take time to pray and commit each of your family members to Jesus, letting them go into His care and letting your faith for each rest in Jesus.

Summary:

As the Totti family drives to a family reunion, Sydney and Sam get talking with their parents about why and how they care for one another in their family. They demonstrate caring by continually passing items back to their little sister. They realize that Jesus cares about their families and that their own acts of caring sometimes take a little effort.

Setting: A family minivan

Props:

- Five chairs
- Handheld electronic game
- Colored markers in a packet
- Sipper cup
- Backpack or canvas bag
- Map
- Paper on a clipboard
- Teddy bear
- Baggie of small crackers

Characters:

- Mr. Edward Totti
- Sydney
- Sophia
- Mrs. Helen Totti
- Sam

Teacher Tip:

Set up the five chairs to look like the interior seating of a minivan, with two forming a front row (space between them), two forming a second row (directly behind the first two), and one in the back (in the center). To allow for the audience to see all the characters, you might set up the seating on an angle to the audience.

Our Family

*As the scene opens, the Totti family is riding in their minivan, parents in front, **Sydney** and **Sam** in the second row, and little **Sophia** in the back. **Mr. Totti** drives, **Sydney** colors with markers on the clipboard, **Sam** plays with the electronic game. The rest of the props are in the bag at **Mrs. Totti's** feet. They all move and jostle a tiny bit the entire time to simulate car movement.*

Sydney: *(Looks up from her coloring.)* Is this family reunion going to be any fun?

Mrs. Totti: *(Speaking over her shoulder.)* Of course, Sydney. Though I don't think you'll know everyone.

Mr. Totti: Helen, which exit do we take?

Mrs. Totti: *(Digs the map out of the bag and elaborately unfolds it and looks it over. Leaves it open on her lap to be in the way as she digs for more things later.)* Hmm, it looks like we might need to take this little highway here to get to 83, which is a frontage road to …

Sydney: *(Ignoring the conversation in the front seat.)* 'Cause, you know, I really don't want to be bored.

Sam: I don't either.

Sophia: *(Shouting to be heard in the front.)* Mommy! Where's my bear-bear?

Mr. Totti: *(Talking over the kids.)* Helen, can you just tell me the exit number?

Mrs. Totti: *(Looks at her husband.)* Twenty-three. *(Looks at **Sydney** and **Sam**.)* You won't be. *(Looks at **Sophia**.)* Just a minute.

Mr. Totti, Sophia, Sydney: *(Together.)* What?

Mrs. Totti: *(Looks at husband).* First of all, Edward, take exit 23. *(She digs in the bag and pulls out a stuffed animal. Reaches to hand it over her shoulder.)* Sam, would you hand this back to your sister, please?

Sam: Why? My hands are full. *(He holds up his game.)*

Mrs. Totti: Sydney, would you pass this back to your sister, please?

Sydney: My hands are full too! *(She holds up her clipboard and markers.)*

Sophia: Bear-bear! I want bear-bear!

Mrs. Totti: Would one of you PLEASE pass this back to your sister?

Sydney: *(Sighs. Sets down her stuff carefully on her lap. Takes the bear and passes it back to **Sophia**, who hugs it.)* Why do you always say "your sister" instead of "Sophia"? I know she's my sister.

Mrs. Totti: Well, it's because she's your sister that you do so much caring for her.

Sophia: *(Shouting.)* Mommy! I'm hungry!

Mrs. Totti: *(Digs through her bag and comes up with a little bag of snacks.)* Sam, would you please pass this back to your sister?

Sam: (*Not even looking up.*) My hands are still full.

Mrs. Totti: But your sister needs your help.

Sam: (*Sighs. Sets down his game, takes the snack, passes it back to **Sophia**.*) Yeah, we do help a lot with our sister.

Mr. Totti: (*Speaking over his shoulder.*) Passing back some things your sister needs helps not only her, it helps your mom, too, who can't reach her. It shows you care.

Sydney: Families seem like a lot of work.

Mrs. Totti: Families can be a lot of work. But it's great work. It's loving work. And it's just what Jesus wants us to do.

Sam: Are we going to have to "work" at this family reunion?

Sophia: (*Shouting.*) Mommy! I'm thirsty!

Mrs. Totti: (*Digs through the bag until she finds the sipper cup. She looks back and forth between **Sydney** and **Sam**, who both sigh and reach for the cup. One of them takes it and passes it back.*) You know that deep down you care about your sister.

Sam and Sydney: (*They look at each other, then their mom.*) Yeah.

Mrs. Totti: And that's great, because Jesus cares about our families and wants us to care too. At this reunion, they'll be some people you don't know very well and others you see a lot. But just like you've been caring about me and helping me care for Sophia, they'll be family there you can care about.

Mr. Totti: Especially old Aunt Emma. Boy, is she a hoot! Wait till you—

Mrs. Totti: (*Glaring at her husband.*) Edward! (*He stops talking and looks sheepish. Then she turns to the kids.*) Even family members like old Aunt Emma need someone to care about them. Jesus already cares about her—and about all our family—so we'll look for ways to care about them too. And I know that most of this family will be looking for ways to care for you!

Sydney: Okay, Mom. That doesn't sound too bad.

Sam: But does anyone care if I finish my game before we get there?

(*All laugh. Lights out.*)

Curtain Call

■ **How did the Totti family show their care for one another?** (*Mrs. Totti cared for by helping with what they needed—directions, toys, snacks. The kids cared by helping their mom.*)

■ **Why should families care about each other, according to Mr. and Mrs. Totti?** (*because Jesus cares about our families*)

■ **In the Bible story, how did Jesus show He cared about the family?** (*He was sad when they were sad. He went to them when one was sick. He used His power to help them.*)

Alphanoids

The class thinks about who they can believe.

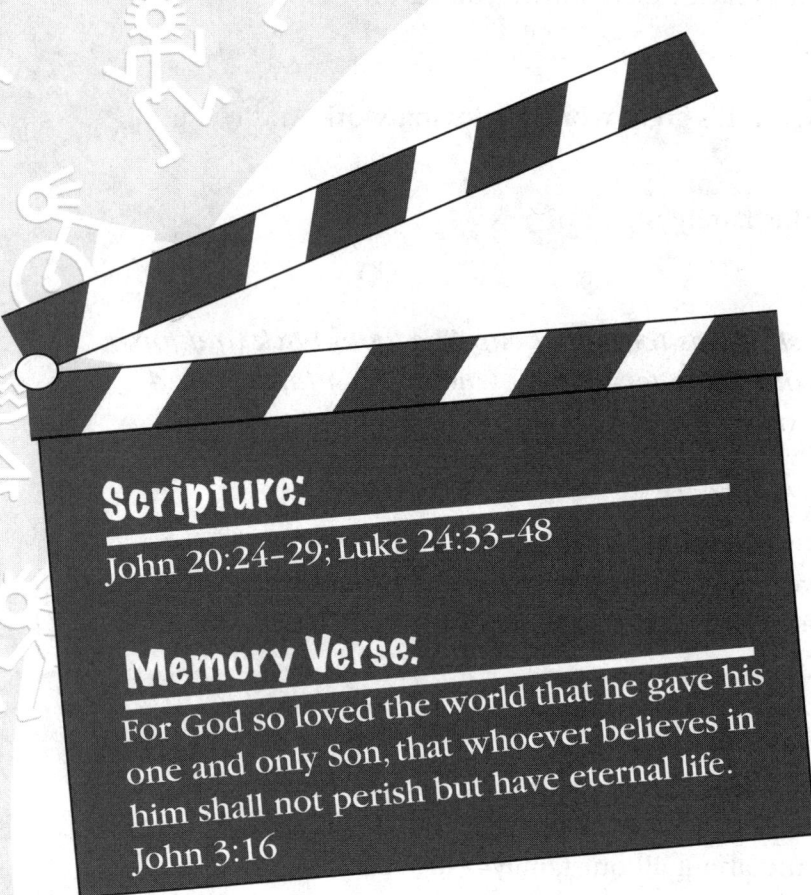

Scripture:

John 20:24–29; Luke 24:33–48

Memory Verse:

For God so loved the world that he gave his one and only Son, that whoever believes in him shall not perish but have eternal life.
John 3:16

Bible Background

When Jesus died, the disciples had a horrible weekend. They feared being arrested themselves, so they hid, possibly in the same room where they had often met with Jesus. When Jesus suddenly appeared before them—in a room that they knew was locked—their first reaction was fright. Both John and Luke record Jesus' first words to His disciples as words of comfort (John 20:19; Luke 24:36).

Thomas's response to Jesus' appearance was one of worship, addressing Him as the sovereign God. Jesus accepted his worship and said: "Because you have seen me, you have believed; blessed are those who have not seen and yet have believed" (John 20:29). Jesus knew those to whom the disciples would preach would not have this opportunity. He did not want us dependent upon only what we see with our own eyes, but rather upon a faith that transcends sight. That's why we're commanded to "live by faith, not by sight" (2 Cor. 5:7).

Today's world is often filled with turmoil and trouble. When turbulence darkens our own lives, we may find ourselves looking to God with doubt in our hearts, asking for a sign so that we can continue to believe. But Jesus already addressed this problem; He knows we have doubts but wants to encourage us to trust Him anyway. Can you remember when times are hard that Jesus is close by you? Can you believe that God can and will answer as He has promised?

Summary:

A visiting actor tries to convince the class that creatures called alphanoids really exist. Rasheen and Mia doubt him, so they question him. Their actions are compared to Thomas in the Bible and how he felt it was ridiculous to believe that Jesus came back to life after He had died. After thinking through who is a reliable source, the kids confirm that the writers of the Gospels can be believed—Jesus is alive!

Setting: A Sunday school classroom

Props:

- Desks or chairs

Characters:

- Rasheen
- Mia
- Mrs. Wise
- Bryan Seachest
- Class (any number of kids)

Teacher Tip:

Whenever you have a skit where the actors are reading their parts (when there isn't time to memorize), remind them to always look up from their scripts to say their lines to the audience. Otherwise, their words will get lost in their papers!

Alphanoids

*As the scene opens, the kids are in their seats, with **Rasheen** and **Mia** near the front.*
***Mrs. Wise** stands in front of them.*

Mrs. Wise: Thomas doubted that Jesus had risen from the dead until Jesus appeared to Him. Jesus wanted Thomas to believe in Him.

*(**Bryan Seachest** runs into the classroom.)*

Bryan Seachest: Alert! Alert! Alphanoids are appearing everywhere. Take cover!

Mrs. Wise: Alphanoids? Who are you?

Bryan Seachest: *(Moves about dramatically whenever he speaks.)* My name is Bryan Seachest, and I am a famous reality TV star. So you can believe what I say. I happened to be at your school when I started seeing the alphanoids dropping from the sky.

*(**Rasheen** hurries to an imaginary window and looks out.)*

Mia: What are alphanoids?

Bryan Seachest: They're green noids from the alpha line.

Rasheen: Well, nothing green is falling from the sky. *(Returns to his seat.)*

Mia: What is a noid?

Rasheen: Yeah, and what's an alpha line?

Bryan Seachest: *(Feigns surprise.)* You don't know? What are you teaching them Mrs. Wise?

Mia: How do you know Mrs. Wise's name?

Bryan Seachest: What a classroom of doubters you are. Are you all doubting Thomases?

Rasheen: Maybe, but you didn't answer the question.

Bryan Seachest: I'm trying to help you. I want you to believe me. What can I do to help you see the danger of our situation?

Mia: *(Jumps up.)* Answer our questions.

Rasheen: *(Jumps up.)* Stop trying to convince us without the facts.

Bryan Seachest: You are doing exactly what Thomas did to Jesus. When the disciples told Thomas that Jesus had risen from the dead, Thomas refused to believe.

Mia: There's a difference.

Bryan Seachest: What's that?

Mia: *(Walks over to Seachest.)* Thomas knew and trusted the other disciples. *(Points at Seachest.)* We don't know you.

Rasheen: *(Joins Mia.)* And Jesus rose from the dead so that Thomas and everyone else would believe in Him. I'm not sure why you're telling us about imaginary alphanoids.

Bryan Seachest: They aren't imaginary. They're about the size of your hand, and they eat homework.

Rasheen: So that's why I don't have my writing homework today.

Mrs. Wise: Rasheen?

Rasheen: Just kidding, Mrs. Wise. I did my writing.

Bryan Seachest: The alphanoids make a "t-t-t" sound—and they are quick. You can almost never see them because they're so fast.

Mia: But you saw them.

Bryan Seachest: That's why I was alarmed. If I saw a couple of them, it means that hundreds of thousands of them must be falling from the sky.

Rasheen: Maybe they turn themselves into the color of the sky, and that's why most people don't see them.

Bryan Seachest: I think you're right.

Mia: Now we know that you aren't telling the truth. At first you said the alphanoids were green. The sky is blue.

Mrs. Wise: *(Laughs.)* Mr. Seachest, I think they caught you. *(She shakes hands with him.)*

Bryan Seachest: You're right. There are no such things as alphanoids. Mrs. Wise asked me to come to class today so you would know what it felt like to be a doubter, like Thomas.

Mrs. Wise: Thomas was told something that seemed too strange for him to believe—Jesus coming back to life.

Bryan Seachest: Jesus wanted Thomas to believe in Him, and He wants you to believe in Him too.

(Lights out.)

Curtain Call

- **In our Bible story, why didn't Thomas believe Jesus had come back to life?** *(He didn't get to see Jesus alive himself; he had to trust the other disciples.)*

- **In the skit, why didn't the kids believe Bryan Seachest?** *(They didn't know him so they didn't know if he could be trusted.)*

- **How can we know that Jesus is alive even though we can't touch Him the way the disciples did?** *(We can see how He answers our prayer. We can know the peace and guidance He gives. We can see how He changes people's lives, etc.)*

Funny Changes

A boy changes outwardly into a clown, but only Jesus changes us on the inside.

Scripture:

Acts 9:1–31

Memory Verse:

Believe in the Lord Jesus,
and you will be saved.

Acts 16:31

Bible Background

Saul was well-educated and had studied under influential and well-known Jewish rabbis of his day. He truly believed that Jesus could not possibly be the expected Messiah and thought he was serving God by silencing or eliminating the "heretical" Jews who believed this. Saul approved of Stephen's death (Acts 8:1) and voted for the executions of other Jewish believers (Acts 26:10). Saul's rage against the early church magnifies the grace of God in the miracle of his conversion.

Damascus was an important trading center, so it would be a place that would spread the message of Jesus further. Damascus was not in Israel, but the Sanhedrin had authority over Jews wherever they lived. Saul was headed to Damascus to arrest people like Ananias. Ironically, God used Ananias to restore Saul's sight.

Initially believers were reluctant to accept the change God brought about in Saul. Ananias and Barnabas were two who put their previous perceptions aside to accept Saul into the fellowship of believers.

Isn't it amazing how God not only changes lives but brings encouragement as well? God is able to change those who are hardhearted. Saul was an avowed enemy of the early church, but God changed him. And God can change the most difficult people you know too.

Do you know someone you believe to be beyond help? It's hard to pray for people like this. But trust God to be greater than any human's stubbornness. Continue to pray for and love this person, and trust God to work in his or her life.

Summary:

Bello the Clown tries to make Bradley like him by giving him his nose, wig, and shoes. So outwardly, Bradley does change after meeting Bello. Bradley's teacher compares those changes to how people change when they meet Jesus—an inward change.

Setting: A classroom

Props:

■ Clown nose
■ Clown wig
■ Clown shoes or oversized adult shoes

Characters:

■ Bello the Clown
■ Teacher
■ Bradley
■ The class (any number)

Teacher Tip:

Set up the scene so that Bello and Bradley will both be facing front when trading costumes. You might set up the class seating (the actors) facing in from the side or at an angle so the audience can see and hear them clearly too.

Funny Changes

*As the scene opens, **Bradley** sits with the class. The **Teacher** stands at the front.*

Teacher: Today we'll have a special guest—Bello the Clown! And once you meet Bello, one of you will be changed!

Bradley: What does that mean?

*(**Bello the Clown** enters, wearing oversized shoes, a wig, and a clown nose.)*

Bello: Hello, kids!

Class: Hello, Bello the Clown.

Bello: I have a question for you, class. What am I?

Class: A clown!

Bello: Are you sure?

Class: Yes!

Bello: Very good. I need a volunteer. *(**Bello** chooses **Bradley**.)* Why don't you stand up front next to me. *(To the class.)* Who is this?

Class: Bradley.

Bello: What is Bradley?

Bradley: I'm a boy.

Bello: Are you sure he's a boy?

Class: Yes!

Bello: Let's see. *(**Bello** takes off his large shoes.)*

Bradley: *(Points to **Bello's** bare feet.)* Your feet aren't enormous. They just look that way with the big shoes on.

Bello: That's right. Let me help you put on these shoes. *(**Bradley** puts on the shoes with **Bello's** help.)* Good. *(**Bello** takes off his wig.)*

Bradley: *(Points to **Bello's** real hair.)* Your hair isn't wild and a crazy color. Your hair looks like other people's hair.

Bello: That's right. Let's put this wig on you. *(**Bello** helps **Bradley** put the wig on.)* Good. *(**Bello** takes off his clown nose.)*

Bradley: *(Points to **Bello's** real nose.)* Your nose is like everyone else's.

Bello: That's right. Let's put this nose on you. (**Bradley** *puts on* **Bello's** *nose.*) Now I have a question for you, class. What am I?

Class: A man.

Bello: Are you sure?

Class: Yes!

Bello: (*Points to* **Bradley.**) Who is this?

Class: A clown.

Bradley: I'm a boy. I'm Bradley.

Bello: Are you sure he's a clown?

Class: Yes!

Teacher: I told you. Once you meet Bello, someone will be changed.

Bradley: I get it. It's like when you believe in Jesus—you're changed. When you meet Bello, you're also changed.

Teacher: Good. The only difference is that Jesus changes you from the inside out.

Bello: I can only change your outside. And that can easily be changed back.

(**Bradley** *gives* **Bello** *the shoes, wig, and nose back so* **Bello** *is a clown again.*)

Teacher: On the outside, Bradley became a clown and Bello became a man. When Jesus changes you, you are different from the inside out.

Bello: Does anyone else want to change into a clown? (*The clown change can continue for each child who wants to try on the clown outfit. Each time this happens, the teacher's last line should be repeated.*)

Curtain Call

- **How did Bradley change?** (*He put on the clown stuff so on the outside he looked like a clown.*)

- **How was Saul's change in our Bible story like this or not like this?** (*Saul didn't change his clothes or hair—he changed inside. Jesus changed how Saul thought about things and how he felt and what he believed.*)

- **How do you think Jesus changes us on the inside?** (*He gives us faith to believe in Him, He helps us see things from His perspective, He helps us understand how to act different, He helps us have self-control, etc.*)

Important Day

The family robot helps a girl figure out what's important each day.

Scripture:

Acts 17

Memory Verse:

All Scripture is God-breathed and is useful for teaching, rebuking, correcting and training in righteousness. 2 Timothy 3:16

Bible Background

One of the trade routes along which Paul shared the Gospel is known as the Egnatian Way, and it included such busy trade centers as Philippi, Amphipolis, Apollonia, Thessalonica, and Berea. By targeting this trade route, Paul knew that the Gospel would be heard by visitors who would take the Good News back to their own towns across the civilized world.

Whenever Paul entered a city, he went first to preach at the synagogue because he knew God's redemptive plan was rooted in the Jewish people (Acts 13:46; Rom. 1:16; 2:9–10). The synagogue provided an audience that knew the Old Testament Scriptures, from which Paul taught about the Messiah. God-fearing Gentiles were also part of the regular audience. Only when the synagogue leaders restricted Paul from speaking or there was no synagogue did Paul take to the public areas.

In Thessalonica, some people were persuaded to believe—both Jews and Gentiles, men and women. But other Jews stirred up trouble for Paul. In Berea, Paul had a more receptive audience, and the Bereans became known for their careful study of the Scriptures and their general acceptance of Paul's teaching about Jesus. In Athens, Paul found great intellectuals to debate with at the Areopagus (an area in Athens also referred to as Mars Hill). But they were more like philosophers who wanted only to discuss any new idea.

Which of these groups do you most relate to? And which do others see in you? Is Bible study a popular notion, or do you take time to carefully and regularly study God's Word?

Summary:

On a holiday called Important Day, Emily gets to do only what is important, under the watchful eye of her robot. Emily finds that things like kickball are optional, but that eating, drinking, and learning about Jesus are important.

Setting: A bedroom

Props:
- Sleeping bag
- Robe

Characters:
- Emily
- Gears (a robot)—speaks in monotone voice, can be dressed in boxes to make him look like a robot

Teacher Tip:

Encourage your actors to look for large motions they can do to always draw the audience's attention to the action onstage.

Important Day

*As the scene opens, **Emily** wakes up on her sleeping bag. She wears a robe. **Gears** enters.*

Emily: Good morning, Gears.

Gears: Happy Important Day, Emily!

Emily: What's Important Day?

Gears: Today you only have to do what is necessary and important. What do you want to do first?

Emily: *(Stands and stretches.)* Maybe I'd better roll up my sleeping bag.

Gears: Cleaning is good, but you don't have to clean today. You don't have to do anything unless it's really, really important.

Emily: That's great. If I don't have to clean, then I'll eat first.

Gears: Yes, you can eat today. Eating is important. You have to eat to stay alive.

Emily: Another important thing is to sleep, but since I just woke up, I won't do that until later tonight.

Gears: Good idea. Rest is important for a growing body. You can do that tonight at bedtime. What would you like to do after you eat?

Emily: After I eat, let's go play kickball. I love playing kickball. *(Acts out running and kicking a ball.)*

Gears: Bzzzzt! *(Makes a buzzer sound and does an out-of-bounds motion with his arms.)* That does not compute. That does not compute.

Emily: What's wrong, Gears? Are you okay?

Gears: Kickball is fun, but it is not one of the most important things in your life.

Emily: But I like kickball. *(Pretends to kick again.)* I can't wait to get out there.

Gears: You can play kickball tomorrow, Emily. You must do important things on Important Day.

Emily: Oh, okay. I guess I have to figure out what's important then.

Gears: Good idea.

Emily: At some point, I'll have to brush my teeth and get dressed.

Gears: Yes. Those are important things to do.

Emily: I suppose you're going to tell me how brushing my teeth keeps cavities away.

Gears: Yes. And putting on clothing keeps you warm and able to go out in public.

Emily: I'll talk to my parents and see if they need me to do anything for them.

Gears: Another good idea. Family relationships are important, and serving others is important too.

Emily: What else is really important?

Gears: Think of only the most important thing.

Emily: *(Paces and thinks.)* TV?

Gears: Bzzzzt! *(Does out-of-bounds motion.)* No.

Emily: *(Paces some more.)* Music?

Gears: Bzzzzt! *(Does out-of-bounds motion.)* No.

Emily: *(Exasperated.)* Crafts?

Gears: Bzzzzt! *(Does out-of-bounds motion.)* No.

Emily: I give up, Gears. What's the most important thing?

Gears: The most important thing you can do today—or any day—is to learn more about Jesus.

Emily: Like I do at Sunday school?

Gears: Check. But you can also learn about Him at home or wherever you go. You can read the Bible, talk to your parents about Jesus, and pray.

Emily: And what if I do that every day?

Gears: Then you make every day a very important day. *(They high-five and exit.)*

Curtain Call

- **If you had a robot, what are some things you think that robot would tell you are important to do?** *(Let volunteers name things, including those named in the skit.)*

- **In our Bible story, what were the important things that Paul and the other Christians did?** *(they studied and learned from the Bible all the time, etc.)*

- **What are ways that you can learn from the Bible?** *(by coming to Sunday school and church, by reading Bible stories at home, by talking with Christians about what the Bible teaches, etc.)*

Your Part

A class needs everyone doing their part to make their story sounds.

Scripture:

Acts 18

Memory Verse:

We are God's workmanship, created in Christ Jesus to do good works.
Ephesians 2:10

Bible Background

Acts 18 gives several examples of people doing their parts for Jesus. None of them were trying to draw attention to themselves; they were just responding to God's work in their lives. Each one used what he or she knew, and each one did something different to spread the Gospel of Christ.

How they ended up where they are found in Acts 18 is an example of their trust in God, as they continued to serve God no matter where they found themselves. In A.D. 49 the Emperor Claudius expelled all Jews from Rome. Claudius's biographer, Suetonius, wrote that the expulsion was to stop riots among the Jews over someone named "Chrestus." Most likely these were disputes over whether Christ was the Messiah. Aquila and Priscilla were among the expelled Jews. They chose to live and work in Corinth.

Apollos was a highly educated Jewish man from Alexandria, Egypt. Aquila and Priscilla understood that Apollos was effectively teaching what he knew about Jesus, but much was missing. Obviously Apollos was receptive of the instruction from Aquila and Priscilla (then at Ephesus). They eventually encouraged Apollos to go to Corinth and wrote a letter of introduction for him.

God is with us in our work. Whatever part we do, wherever we find ourselves, Jesus will use our work for Him, along with what others do, to accomplish what He desires. The outcome belongs to the Lord; we are only responsible to do our part. What can you do for the Lord today?

Summary:

A class forms a tiger's growl by holding up papers with a giant G and R on them, each child having just a piece of a letter. But Jamie goes off with Carlos to goof off elsewhere in the room. So as the teacher reads the story and it's time for the tiger to growl, it appears that the kids hold up a G and P—because Jamie who is missing holds the slanted "leg" of the R. And "GP" doesn't sound at all like a growl! Jamie and Carlos learn that everyone has a part, no matter how small, both in the classroom and when serving Jesus.

Setting: A classroom

Props:

- Black marker
- Scissors
- Butcher paper or poster board
- To make the sign, draw a giant G and R on butcher paper, darkening and widening the lines to be easy for the audience to read. Cut each letter into four parts. Be sure when you cut the R that each "leg" is on its own sheet.

Characters:

- Teacher
- Jamie
- Six more students
- Carlos
- Ally

Teacher Tip:

Have your actors practice ahead of time holding up their papers together to form the two letters.

Your Part

*As the scene opens, eight kids have sheets of paper marked with parts of the G and R. The **teacher** stands to one side of them so the audience will be able to read the papers when held up. **Jamie** holds onto his paper—the slanted "leg" of the R—and goes to the other side of the room to goof off with **Carlos**.*

Teacher: Today, kids, you are going to help me tell a story about a terrible tiger. What sound does a tiger make? It growls! So every time you hear the word growl, hold your papers up to form the letters G and R and read what is on them. Are you ready?

Kids: Yes!

Teacher: Once upon a time, there was a terrible tiger with a grumpy growl.

(The seven kids by the teacher hold up papers together to form the letters G and P— because the slanted leg of the R is missing. The sound the kids make will sound like "gip, gip" rather than "grr, grr.")

Kids: GP. GP. GP. GP. GP. *(After making the "gip" sound, kids put their papers back down.)*

Teacher: *(Looks confused.)* That's not how a tiger growls.

Kids: *(They respond by holding up the papers together again, showing the letters G and P.)* GP. GP. GP. GP. GP. *(Then they lower their papers.)*

Teacher: Something's really wrong. Kids, please hold up your papers again.

Kids: *(Hold up the papers together, showing the letters G and P.)* GP. GP. GP. GP. GP.

Teacher: *(Reads their papers.)* Does that say, "GP"? Where is the kid who should be holding the paper that make our P into an R?

Ally: He's over there with Carlos. *(Points off to the side.)*

Teacher: Jamie! Carlos! Come over here, please.

*(**Carlos** and **Jamie** come over.)*

Teacher: What are you doing?

Carlos: Just playing.

Teacher: Why aren't you with the rest of us?

Jamie: My job isn't that important. Anyone can hold a sheet of paper in the air.

Carlos: We didn't think anyone would miss Jamie.

Ally: But your part is really important.

Teacher: Everyone's part is important, no matter how small it seems.

Carlos: I don't understand.

Teacher: Let's show them, kids. Are you ready?

Kids: Yes!

Teacher: Once upon a time, there was a terrible tiger with a grumpy growl.

Kids: *(Kids hold their pieces of papers to form G and P.)* GP. GP. GP. GP. GP. *(Then they lower their papers.)*

Jamie: That's not how a tiger growls.

Kids: *(Raise papers again.)* GP. GP. GP. GP. GP. *(Lower papers.)*

Teacher: Correct, but it's how our tiger growls.

Kids: *(Raise papers.)* GP. GP. GP. GP. GP. *(Lower their papers.)*

Teacher: At least, that's how it growls if your sheet of paper is not where it belongs. Everyone in our class has a part to play, just as every person has some part in God's family. Why don't you get in place and do your part, and then we can get on with the story?

(Jamie joins the kids holding letters while Carlos joins the audience.)

Teacher: Once upon a time, there was a terrible tiger with a grumpy growl.

Kids: *(Everyone holds up their papers together to form G and R.)* Gr. Gr. Gr. Gr. Gr.

(Teacher and kids cheer.)

Teacher: We can each do our part in our class and for Jesus.

Curtain Call

■ **What did Carlos and Jamie think of the part Jamie had to play?** *(that Jamie's piece of paper wasn't important)*

■ **What small but important things were done in our Bible story?** *(Aquila and Priscilla helped teach Apollos about something he didn't know, and they wrote a letter for him when he left.)*

■ **Can you think of little things that are important to do?** *(help another kid with a chore or responsibility, explain something to someone who doesn't understand what to do, share something, etc.)*

Show You Care

A game show challenges contestants to think of ways
to show they care about others.

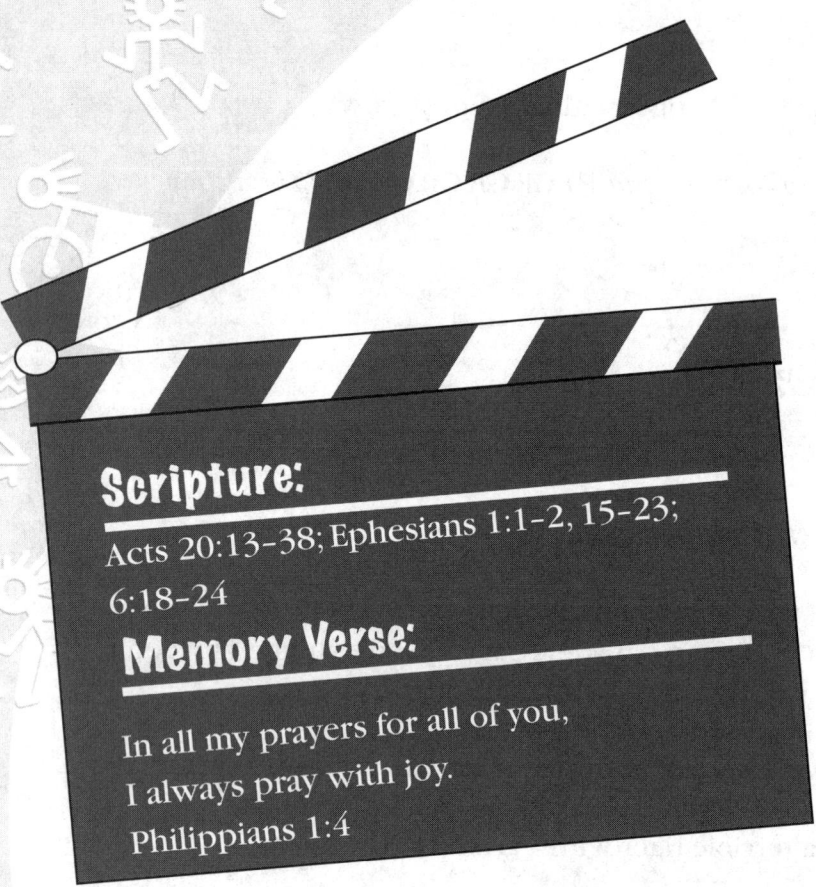

Scripture:
Acts 20:13–38; Ephesians 1:1–2, 15–23;
6:18–24

Memory Verse:

In all my prayers for all of you,
I always pray with joy.
Philippians 1:4

Bible Background

When Paul was imprisoned in
Rome, he kept contact with the
various churches he had helped
found by writing letters to
them. Ephesians is one of four
surviving letters written during
this time. Actually, the phrase found in the first verse of Ephesians, "in Ephesus," is not found
in some of the earliest Greek manuscripts. Paul's correspondence was probably sent as a
circular letter to several area churches, of which Ephesus was the most important. This would
explain why there are few personal greetings in Ephesians as compared with Romans and
1 Corinthians.

Before being imprisoned, Paul went to Jerusalem; he was convinced that was what God
wanted. He was willing to complete the mission God gave him even at the expense of his
own life (Acts 20:24). When Paul was put on trial and then sent to Rome and confined to
house arrest, he realized he was limited in what he could do for others. But Paul still knew
that he could show his care for others by praying for them.

Showing we care about others by praying for them overcomes all obstacles. Prayer can fit
into busy schedules and overcome any physical limitations that close us in. The power of God's
response to our prayers is not limited by the obstacles we face. God's answers to our prayers
are not confined by prison walls, dangerous situations, or boundaries between races, cultures,
and nations. Show those you care about how much you really care by taking time to pray
for them.

Summary:

The game show host of "Show You Care" gives Rodney and Isabel different situations, and these two kids must explain what they would do in those situations to show they care. The final conclusion is that praying shows others they care and makes them winners.

Setting: A game show

Props:

- Table for contestants to stand behind
- Two buzzers or bells

Characters:

- Game Show Host
- Rodney
- Isabel

Teacher Tip:

Encourage your actors to get into their characters and think of ways to express those parts—even going overboard for comedic effect.

Show You Care

*As the scene opens, the **Game Show Host** faces contestants **Rodney** and **Isabel**, who face the audience. They are standing behind a table, and each has a buzzer or bell.*

Host: Hello, ladies and gentlemen, and welcome to our game show, "Show You Care," where kids must decide what they would do to show they care. Let me introduce today's contestants. Rodney is a student from Cronkers. Let's give Rodney a warm welcome. *(Leads the audience in clapping.)*

Rodney: *(Waves to audience.)* Thank you. I'm glad to be here, and I love playing games.

Host: Isabel is a student from Jesmit. Let's give a warm welcome to Isabel. *(Claps.)*

Isabel: *(Smiles and speaks excitedly.)* Thank you, Mr. Game Show Host. I was so excited to win the chance to be on your show. I'm just so excited! Really excited!

Host: Are you both ready to play "Show You Care"?

Rodney and Isabel: Yes!

Host: Then let's get started. Your first question: How could you show a sick person that you care? *(**Rodney** buzzes.)* Rodney?

Rodney: I'd give him chicken soup.

Host: Great answer, Rodney! Chicken soup or any food that helps someone get well shows you care. You get 100 points. *(Everyone claps. **Rodney** waves and bows in mock humility.)*

Rodney: Really? That was just a guess. I had no idea that chicken soup would help make someone feel better. Since the person's sick, I thought I'd have the TV remote all to myself, so I'd want to eat something yummy while watching my favorite shows. Since I'm eating chicken soup, I thought I'd give the sick person some too. Then I don't have to waste my time by making him something else to eat.

Host: Hmm, your motivation doesn't sound right, but your answer was. Let's move on to the next question: If a soldier was lonely because he was far away from his family, how could you show you care? *(**Rodney** buzzes.)* Rodney?

Rodney: Nothing. He's far away, and I can only cross a couple of streets near my house if I have my parents' permission. So I guess the soldier would be on his own.

Host: That is an incorrect answer. Isabel, you have a chance to buzz and give an answer.

Isabel: *(Buzzes.)* Well, if there was a lonely soldier my family knew, I would write him a letter and ask my parents if we could send him a care package.

Host: Super answer, Isabel! Writing letters and sending care packages are two great ways to show someone far away that you care. You get 100 points. *(Everyone claps.)*

Isabel: *(Jumps up and down, excited.)* Oh, boy! Thank you, I'm so excited!

Host: Now the scores are tied. You each have 100 points. Okay, here's our final question to decide the winner of today's game. Are you ready?

Rodney: Bring it on!

Isabel: I'm ready! I'm so excited!

Host: Remember that your answer has to be something that you can do at your age. Now for the question: When you hear about a missionary from your church who is working in a dangerous place to tell others about Jesus, how can you show you care? *(**Rodney** buzzes.)* Rodney?

Rodney: I'd hop on a plane and fly over there and use my karate that I learned in my weekly karate class to beat up any bad guys. *(Steps out and throws some karate kicks in the air.)* Ai-yah! *(Returns to his spot and grins broadly as if he's already won the game.)*

Host: Um, Rodney, do you remember I said it had to be something you could really do?

Rodney: Yeah, what's wrong with that? I can really do karate!

Host: Well, think of it this way. Would your parents let a kid your age hop on a plane and fly overseas and fight terrorists? I don't think so. And besides, the kind of danger that missionaries find themselves in isn't always what you think. There are many different kinds of danger.

Rodney: Oh, rats. *(Slumps.)*

Isabel: *(Buzzes.)* Can I answer? *(**Host** nods.)* I would pray for the missionary because from this far away, that's the very best way to help them.

Host: That's the answer we were looking for! Congratulations, Isabel! You're a winner! *(Walks over and shakes **Rodney's** hand and then **Isabel's**.)* Do you have any words for our audience?

Isabel: Well, there are lots of ways to show you care about someone. Rodney had a good one at the start. But a great way to care for anyone you know is to pray for them.

Host: That's right, audience. Prayer shows you care for each other! Thanks for playing "Show You Care."

Curtain Call

- **How did the kids on the game show say they could show they care?** *(by doing things to help people feel better and, most importantly, by praying)*

- **In our Bible story, Paul was too far away to do much for the people he cared about. What did he do to show he cared?** *(He prayed and wrote them letters.)*

- **Who are people you could pray for?** *(Let volunteers name people they know.)*

God's Got You Covered

Just as clothes protect in harsh weather, God's got us covered too.

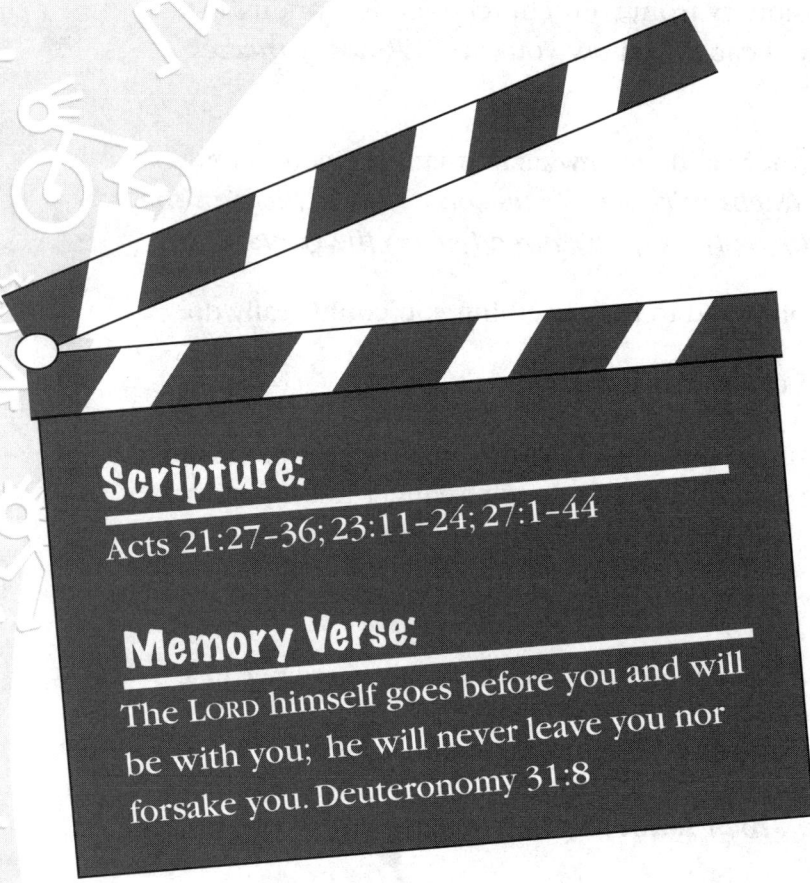

Scripture:

Acts 21:27–36; 23:11–24; 27:1–44

Memory Verse:

The LORD himself goes before you and will be with you; he will never leave you nor forsake you. Deuteronomy 31:8

Bible Background

The Lord told Paul that he would preach in Rome (Acts 23:11). He got there by invoking his right as a Roman citizen to an appeal before Caesar after he was convicted in Jerusalem, so he was transported to Rome (Acts 25:11). But his journey along the way created a new chapter in his life—and several chapters in the Bible.

Sailing was dangerous in the winter months during Bible times. But the captain wanted to make progress, and he decided to leave in the fall and try to reach Rome before the worst of winter weather set in. The ship was repeatedly blown off course or delayed at unintended harbors. They ended up being shipwrecked on the island of Malta.

It was most likely Paul's faith in God and calm assurance of God's power that brought Paul into prominence. The Roman centurion followed Paul's advice on several matters, including not following the standard practice of killing all prisoners to prevent escape during a chaotic evacuation.

We often are assured of God's plans for us, and we work to follow those plans. Yet sometimes the Lord has unexpected learning experiences for us along the way. During these unforeseen and troubling times, stand firm on God's promises and "keep up your courage" just as Paul did on the ship careening toward Malta (Acts 27:21–26). God is always with you in hard times. Keep trusting and praying until the winds of your life turn favorable again. Then keep trusting and praying through the sunny times too!

Summary:

Tanesha learns that she must use a coat, hat, snow pants, gloves, boots, and a scarf to cover her body as she goes outside in snowy weather. With reminders from her dad, she learns that God's got her covered, especially in hard times.

Setting: A home

Props:

- Coat
- Gloves
- Boots
- Hat
- Snow pants
- Scarf

Characters:

- Dad
- Tanesha

Teacher Tip:

If you choose, the actor can pantomime putting on the winter gear, so choose an actor who is comfortable working with nvisible props!

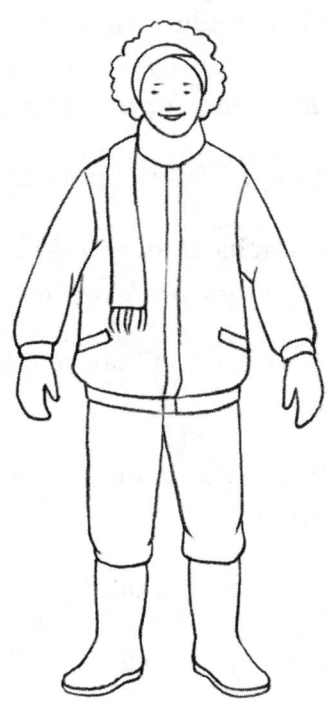

God's Got You Covered

*As the scene opens, **Tanesha** is by an imaginary door. **Dad** is offstage where he can be heard by the audience. A pile of winter wear is on the side of the stage area.*

Tanesha: *(Pretending to look out a window.)* Wow, look at that storm! It's like a blizzard! But I promised I'd go down the street to Alexandra's and help her with her project. *(Pretends to open the door and then be blown back; then she pretends to slam the door shut.)* Phew!

Dad: *(Voice calling from offstage.)* Tanesha! Don't forget to bundle up!

Tanesha: *(To self.)* No kidding. *(Calls back to her **Dad**.)* Okay, Dad! I got it covered! *(She grabs a coat from the pile and pulls it on, neglecting to button it. She opens the door again and is again blown back by the wind. She slams the door shut.)* Wow!

Dad: *(Voice from offstage.)* Tanesha! Don't forget to button up tight! You've got to be covered up!

Tanesha: *(To self.)* Hmm, not bad advice. *(Calling to **Dad**.)* Good idea! I guess I was too excited about going. I got it covered now! *(She buttons up tight. Then she opens the door, gets caught by a gust of wind, and slams the door shut.)* Oh, man. Am I ready for this?

Dad: *(Voice from offstage.)* Tanesha! Don't forget to wear a hat. You need to keep your head covered.

Tanesha: *(Calling back to **Dad**.)* Okay, I have my hat. *(Roots through the pile to find a hat, puts it on securely. Goes to the door, opens it, gets blown, slams it.)*

Dad: *(Voice from offstage.)* And Tanesha! Be sure to put on snow pants! You need to keep covered in this weather!

Tanesha: *(To self.)* Is he reading my mind? How can he see me from the next room? *(Hollers.)* Okay, Dad! *(Looks through the pile for snow pants, then pulls them on. Again she opens the door, gets blown, and slams it shut.)*

Dad: *(Voice from offstage.)* Snow boots, Tanesha! Ordinary shoes won't do the job!

Tanesha: *(Hollers.)* Gotcha, Dad! *(Looks for the boots, then pulls them on. Goes to the door, opens it, gets blown, slams it. Speaks aloud to self.)* This isn't as easy as it looks.

Dad: *(Voice from offstage.)* Wait, Tanesha! Are you wearing gloves? You don't want your uncovered hands to freeze.

Tanesha: *(To self.)* Well, I was going to skip it, but . . . *(Digs through pile, puts on gloves, repeats the scene at the door.)*

Dad: *(Hollers.)* Are you covered up now?

Tanesha: *(Hollers.)* I thought I was! But I keep learning I'm not! At least, not enough for this terrible weather!

Dad: *(Hollers.)* One more thing! Grab a scarf!

Tanesha: *(Hollers.)* I don't even like scarves! But I'll do it. *(She roots through the pile and finds a scarf to put on. Then she stands and stares at the door. Speaks to self.)* Okay, I have a coat—well-buttoned—a hat, snow pants, boots, gloves, and a scarf. I'm ready for the terrible weather.

Dad: *(Enters.)* Ah, Tanesha, you look well covered up!

Tanesha: I'm definitely covered, Dad.

Dad: There's one more thing you need.

Tanesha: What? If I put on anything else, I'll fall over!

Dad: *(Laughs.)* This thing doesn't weigh much. You need to take God's covering with you.

Tanesha: God's covering? What do you mean?

Dad: Just like all these things cover you and keep you safe in bad weather, God also covers you—with His protection, with His love—during hard times. And that doesn't mean just during hard winter storms.

Tanesha: That sounds like something else I sure could use. Just looking at that storm makes me want a reminder that God is close by.

Dad: Well, let this pile of winter clothes you're wearing remind you. God is with you in good times and bad. He's got you covered in every hard time.

Tanesha: Thanks, Dad. *(Sighs.)* But do you think I could go now? It's getting hot in here!

Dad: *(He chuckles and opens the door.* **Tanesha** *forces her way into the wind and off-stage.* **Dad** *hollers out the door after her.)* God's got you covered!

(Lights out.)

Curtain Call

- **How was Paul able to stay calm in the midst of the storm at sea?** *(He trusted what God had told him. He knew God would keep His word.)*

- **What did Tanesha have to do to deal with harsh weather? Why?** *(cover up in all kinds of winter clothes so she wouldn't be cold or get frostbitten)*

- **What else did Tanesha's dad say she needed?** *(God's covering—to remember that God is with her in the harsh weather and in hard times)*

- **What kinds of hard things do you face? Which of those times is God with you?** *(Let volunteers share. Emphasize that God is with them in every situation.)*

Ig-pay Atin-lay

A bit of pig-Latin "translation" teaches that people need to hear about Jesus.

Scripture:

Acts 25:23–27; 26; Mark 16:15

Memory Verse:

Go into all the world and preach the good news to all creation.

Mark 16:15

Bible Background

King Herod Agrippa II, appointed by the Roman emperor, ruled north of Judea. His sister, Bernice, was married to Governor Festus, who was struggling to establish his rule of Judea. When the Jewish leaders brought charges against Paul, Festus was in charge of the verdict. He could have released Paul, but that would have been politically unpopular. Since Agrippa and Bernice were visiting, Festus conveniently passed the buck, knowing that he could pass on their comments to Rome and so remove the blame for any bad decisions from himself. After hearing Paul, all three knew that the problem of Paul was best ignored and sent to Rome. While humans intended to pass along a "problem," God used the opportunity for Paul to preach to Caesar himself.

Paul continually looked for opportunities to tell others about Jesus. He shared with Jews and Gentiles, men and women, rich and poor, rulers and guards. No matter how often or in what ways Paul's mission to spread the Good News was "interrupted," Paul used every opportunity to tell others about Jesus.

As followers of Jesus, we share in the responsibility to spread the Good News wherever and whenever God gives us opportunity. As you prayerfully prepare for this lesson, ask God to make you aware of the "interruptions" He brings to your life. Trust Him to help you share in the spreading of the Good News to your family, neighborhood, workplace, or countries across the globe.

Summary:

When a thirsty student speaks only in pig Latin, Anna must translate so Brogan can give the student a cup of water. Brogan begins to understand how important it is to talk to people in their own language so they can understand what Jesus did.

Setting: A lunchroom

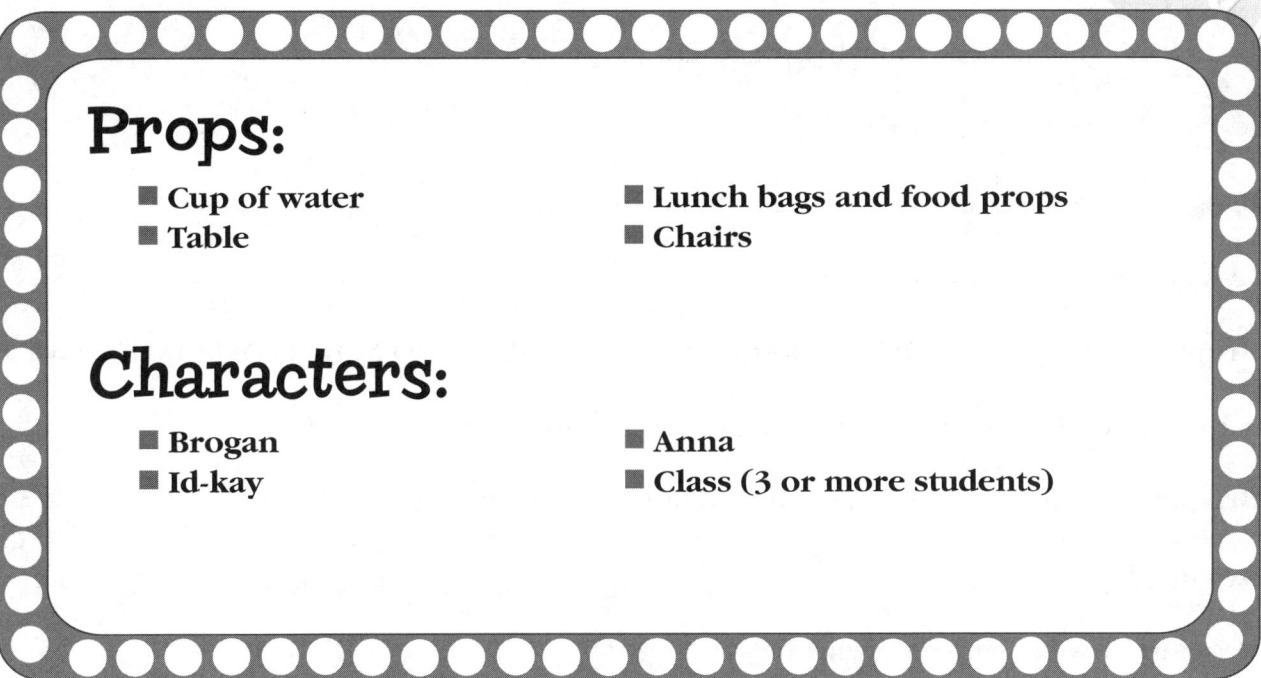

Props:

- Cup of water
- Table
- Lunch bags and food props
- Chairs

Characters:

- Brogan
- Id-kay
- Anna
- Class (3 or more students)

Teacher Tip:

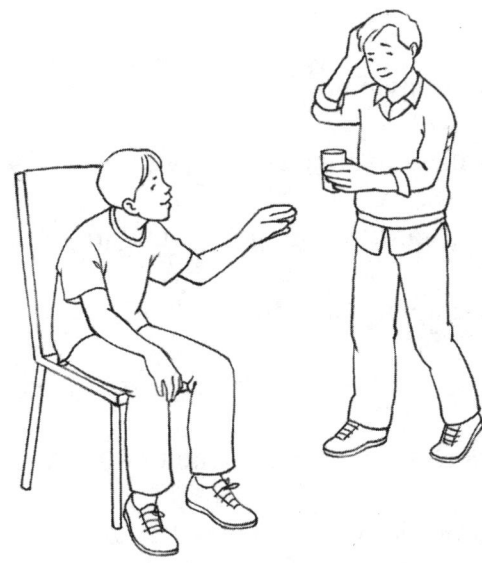

Pig Latin is pronounced by taking the first sound of each word and putting it at the end of the word, followed by "ay." So "pig" is "ig-pay," and "latin" is "atin-lay." One-syllable words or words beginning with a vowel are often pronounced the right way with the "ay" sound simply added to the end. The pig Latin in this skit is written as simply as possible to make it easy for elementary kids.

Ig-pay Atin-lay

*As the scene opens, the **Class**, **Brogan**, and **Anna** are eating lunch. **Id-kay** enters and sits on an empty chair. He appears out of breath and tired.*

Id-kay: Ater-way, ease-play.

Brogan: What?

Id-kay: I-ay eed-nay ater-way, ease-play.

Brogan: I don't understand what you're saying.

Id-kay: I-ay eed-nay ater-way.

Brogan: *(Speaking louder)* What do you need?

Id-kay: I-ay eed-nay ater-way.

Brogan: *(Loudly and slowly, emphasizing each syllable)* I DO NOT UNDERSTAND YOU!

Anna: Quiet, Brogan. He's speaking a different language. He's not deaf.

Brogan: But he needs something, and I don't know what it is.

Anna: I do.

Brogan: How do you know what he's saying?

Anna: Because I speak fluent pig Latin. *(To **Id-kay**.)* Y-may ame-nay is-ay Nana-ay.

Brogan: What did you say?

Anna: I told him my name.

Brogan: Your name is that long in pig Latin?

Anna: No, silly. I said, "My name is Anna" in pig Latin.

Id-kay: Y-may ame-nay is-ay Id-kay.

Anna: *(To **Brogan**)* He says his name is Id-kay.

Brogan: I've never heard that name before. Ask him if he's hurt.

Id-kay: I-ay nunder-stand-ay ou-yay. I-ay am-ay ot-nay urt-hay.

Anna: He says he understands you. He says he's not hurt.

Brogan: Then what's wrong?

Id-kay: I-ay eed-nay ater-way. Ease-play.

Brogan: What did he say? It's the same words he used earlier.

Anna: He says he needs water. He's thirsty.

Brogan: Is that all? *(**Brogan** pushes a glass of water to Id-kay, who drinks it.)*

Id-kay: Ank-thay ou-yay! *(**Id-kay** exits.)*

Brogan: I'm sure glad you understand pig Latin.

Anna: It's really pretty easy. You just take the first sound of a word, put it at the end of the word, and add "ay" to it. When I grow up, I want to be a translator—you know, a person who tells people what other people are saying in another language.

Brogan: That's an important job. People all over the world need to hear about Jesus. If we can't speak their language, we can't tell them about Him. If you translate for them, they can read the Bible in their own language.

Anna: That'd be fun to do.

Brogan: I want to understand what people are saying, even if all they want is a glass of water. Maybe I could start by learning hog Latin.

Anna: Not hog—pig Latin. I'd be glad to teach you.

Brogan: I think it's time to line up. Maybe you can give me my first lesson on the playground.

Anna: Kay-oay. *(They stand and line up.)*

Brogan: This is great. Just imagine getting to tell other people all over the world about Jesus. I can't wait! *(**Brogan** exits.)*

Curtain Call

- **Who was Paul able to share the Gospel message with as a result of his imprisonment?** *(Festus, Agrippa, Bernice, his guards, and eventually Caesar)*

- **What was Id-kay's challenge?** *(He needed water, and Brogan couldn't understand him.)*

- **What did Brogan learn?** *(that it's good to speak another language, that if he spoke another language, he could help people learn about Jesus)*

- **Can you name some missionaries you know about? How do they help people learn about Jesus?** *(Let kids share about missionaries they know of from church or whom their parents support.)*

A Cheerful Giver

When a sock separates from her BFF, nothing goes right
until she learns to give unselfishly.

Scripture:

2 Corinthians 8—9

Memory Verse:

God loves a cheerful giver.
2 Corinthians 9:7

Bible Background

Two of Paul's letters to the church in Corinth survived to be added to the canon. It's obvious from the second letter that the church had carefully read and responded to Paul's first letter. He wrote both letters to clarify their questions, to defend his authority as an apostle, and to refute false teachers.

Paul was on his third missionary journey and had been collecting money from Gentile churches in the area to help the impoverished Jewish believers in Jerusalem. The believers in Corinth had previously committed to help that church as well. Paul uses chapters 8 and 9 to encourage follow-through on the Corinthians' commitment. He reminds his readers that they already excel in many Christian graces, and he encourages them to excel in the grace of giving as well.

Compared to the churches in Macedonia, which had put together a large donation, the believers in Corinth were financially well-off. Corinth was one of the most prosperous cities in Greece, largely because of its strategic location in the center of trade between the east and west.

Whether we are upper-middle-class or low-income or somewhere in between, the joy of giving financially is a tremendous joy and obligation, according to Scripture. It takes a lot of faith to give to God's work, especially if it doesn't directly benefit our own congregation or ministries, but that makes the gift all the more unselfish. Take time to periodically reexamine your giving, and ask God for a cheerful heart in this matter.

Summary:

Left Sock at first relishes the freedom of finally being alone, without its BFF (Best Friend Forever) Right Sock. It wants some selfish time alone and won't help Right Sock, much less give cheerfully to do its job. But Left Sock discovers that it can't walk or hold a conversation or have fun sliding by itself. When Right Sock comes, Left Sock decides to be a cheerful giver and do its job well.

Setting: Anywhere

Props:

- Two adult-size white crew socks, decorated to look like simple sock puppets (even just two large drawn-on eyes would work)
- Large sign labeled "Land of Clothing" to hang beside or behind the Student

Characters:

- Narrator
- Left Sock
- Student
- Right Sock

Teacher Tip:

If you don't have microphones for the Socks, have those actors stand where they can be clearly heard by the audience, even if they aren't completely hidden.

A Cheerful Giver

*As the scene opens, the **student** stands by large sign labeled "Land of Clothing," and puts a large sock on her left foot and wiggles it to move like a mouth. Whenever **Left Sock** speaks, the **student** holds up that foot with the sock and moves its "mouth" to show it talking. When **Right Sock** enters, the **student** puts on the other sock and moves its mouth in the same manner. The voices for the **Socks** and **Narrator** should come from offstage or a part of the room where the audience can clearly hear but not be obviously seen.*

Narrator: In the Land of Clothing lived a sock who was excited to be on her own.

Left Sock: I'm excited to be on my own!

Narrator: Left Sock always had to do her job with her BFF—Best Friend Forever—Right Sock.

Left Sock: I wonder what my BFF Right Sock is doing.

Narrator: They always worked together to do their job, but Left Sock got tired of it.

Left Sock: I was tired of working. I was tired of never being on my own. Whenever I went for a walk, my BFF Right Sock was always there. When I talked, my BFF Right Sock was always there. When I played and slid, Right Sock was always there. But not now. Now I finally get to do things my way.

Narrator: Left Sock was very proud of herself.

Left Sock: I'm very proud of myself.

Narrator: But there was a problem in the Land of Clothing.

Left Sock: I think I'll go for a walk.

*(**Student** hops on left foot awkwardly.)*

Left Sock: Ow! Oooo! Ouch! Stop that. That hurts. That's not walking. *(**Student** stops hopping.)*

Narrator: Left Sock realized that she couldn't walk unless her BFF Right Sock was with her. She couldn't do anything, much less her job of helping feet walk.

Left Sock: Forget the walking. I really don't like doing that job alone. *(Pauses.)* Hmm, I think I'll have a conversation. *(Pauses, clears throat.)* How are you doing today?

Narrator: But no one answered Left Sock. She couldn't have a conversation without her BFF Right Sock.

Left Sock: I can't do that alone either. Hmm, I think I'll just have some fun then. I'll go slip and slide. *(**Student** attempts to slide around the floor on left foot.)* Whee! *(Stumbles.)* Um, whee? *(Straightens up.)* Boy, this is hard. Lemme try again. *(Slides on one foot again.)* Whee! *(Trips.)* Humpf. This isn't working.

Narrator: Left Sock realized she couldn't have fun sliding unless her BFF Right Sock was with her.

Left Sock: What am I going to do? I can't walk. I can't talk. I can't have fun at all without my BFF! Doing things my own way seems pretty selfish now. Maybe I should have tried to be more cheerful doing my job with Right Sock.

Narrator: So Left Sock had a change of heart and decided to be a cheerful giver.

Left Sock: *(Calling.)* Right Sock! Right Sock! Where are you?

(The second sock puppet is thrown onstage from offstage. **Student** *puts it on the right foot. The* **two socks** *face each other to talk.)*

Right Sock: Hey, there!

Left Sock: My best friend forever! There you are! I missed you! *(The* **two socks** *"hug.")* How have you been?

Right Sock: Not so good. I couldn't do anything without you! Worst of all, I couldn't do my job without you.

Left Sock: I couldn't do anything without you either. I feel really bad now.

Right Sock: Will you come back?

Left Sock: Yes, and I promise: I'll not only stick around and do my job, I'll do it cheerfully.

Right Sock: I'm glad to have you back, BFF. I'm glad to hear you're going to give cheerfully to our work.

Narrator: God loves a cheerful giver.

Left Sock: Let's walk! *(***Student** *walks.)*

Right Sock: And slide! *(***Student** *slides smoothly offstage.)*

Narrator: Everything in the Land of Clothing was happy again.

Curtain Call

■ **What kind of givers did Paul encourage the Corinthians to be?** *(cheerful, joyful, willing, etc.)*

■ **What went wrong with Left Sock?** *(She didn't want to do her job with Right Sock cheerfully. She wanted to do things her own way.)*

■ **How did Left Sock figure out the problem?** *(Nothing went right when she was by herself, and she didn't end up being happy.)*

■ **What are ways you can give cheerfully?** *(Help the kids think through ways they can give cheerfully of themselves.)*

The Care Package

A Christian teacher taught the kids to give and pray;
now here's their chance to practice.

Scripture:

Ephesians 4:11–16

Memory Verse:

Obey your leaders and
submit to their authority.
Hebrews 13:17a

Bible Background

After three years of working with the Ephesian church on one of his missionary journeys, Paul was very close to the Christians in Ephesus. While imprisoned in Rome, he wrote them a letter. Paul's aim in the letter was to strengthen and encourage the church there. In Ephesians 4, Paul instructs these Christians to work at being unified, and he outlines spiritual gifts that are to be used in building up and equipping the church body.

These gifts of service were given to believers by Jesus Himself (Eph. 4:7–11). Jesus' purpose in the giving of these gifts was for His people to be prepared to serve Him and grow together into spiritual maturity as they learned about Him. He wanted His people to become mature believers, experiencing all that He has planned for those who love Him. The Ephesian letter focuses on leadership gifts, because Paul knew that strong leaders make a strong church. By focusing on pastors, teachers, and evangelists, Paul was instructing the whole congregation to honor and learn from these leaders, and so build up the whole body.

As a teacher of elementary students, you are building up the body of Christ. These kids look up to you and trust you, and they will follow your Christian example. As a leader, take time to get to know your students, and plan regular times to pray for them. The Holy Spirit will strengthen you in the rough moments and give you joy in your service. Christian leaders—that's you!—help others grow closer to Jesus.

Summary:

Mr. Wittie, the substitute Sunday school teacher, helps the class prepare a care package for Miss Bassett, their regular teacher, who is spending the summer teaching at an overseas Christian camp for kids who haven't heard about Jesus. Stephanie doesn't take much interest in the project, but the others remind her that Miss Bassett has taught them that a way to serve God is to serve other Christians. Stephanie is sad she hasn't brought anything to contribute to the care package. Then she remembers that Miss Bassett taught and showed them that prayer is important, so she decides to add prayers to the package. Mr. Wittie leads the class in praying to "fill" the box.

Setting: Sunday school room

Props:

- Table
- Book
- Large cardboard box with "Airmail" written across the side
- Packing bubbles or foam peanuts
- Bag of hard candies
- Small rubber bouncy balls
- Other items kids might send in a care package, such as pencils, pads, hair bands, etc.

Characters:

- Mr. Wittie
- Varsha
- Austin
- Stephanie
- Class (two or three other kids)

Teacher Tip:

Have all the characters with speaking parts stand behind the table, facing the audience, so they can be clearly heard. Any extra class members should stand not in front of the table, where they would block the audience's view, but on the side.

The Care Package

*As the scene opens, **Mr. Wittie**, **Varsha**, **Austin**, and the class are gathered around a box on a table in the Sunday school room. Other props are spread out on the table. **Stephanie** sits reading a book off to the side.*

Mr. Wittie: *(Holding up the bag of hard candies.)* And who brought this?

Varsha: I did. Miss Bassett wrote us that she wanted something to give to the kids at the overseas summer camp. They're too poor to afford treats like that.

Mr. Wittie: That's a great idea, Varsha. You read Miss Bassett's e-mail pretty carefully.

Austin: *(Bouncing one of the bouncy balls.)* Wish I could keep this. It's fun.

Varsha: Yeah, and because it's fun, we're sending it.

Austin: Okay. I bet the kids at Miss Bassett's summer camp will like playing with it too.

Stephanie: *(Looks up from her book.)* When are we going to start our Sunday school lesson? And I don't want our class to run long because my favorite team is playing on TV right after church.

Mr. Wittie: Hey, Stephanie, this IS our lesson today.

Stephanie: What? Packing a box?

Austin: *(Picks up the box to show it to **Stephanie**.)* This is our care package for Miss Bassett. *(Sets the box back on the table.)*

Varsha: You know she's spending the summer overseas, working in a Christian camp for kids who have never heard about Jesus.

Stephanie: *(Stands up.)* I know that already.

Austin: Didn't you read her e-mail? She asked us to send her some things she can use with the kids there.

Mr. Wittie: The Christian camp provides Bibles and meals and other things they need, but stuff for the kids to play with—that's harder to get.

Varsha: So after the e-mail, we all brought something to put in the care package today. *(All the **kids** shake their heads in agreement.)*

Austin: What did you bring, Stephanie?

Stephanie: *(Walks to the table, looking uncomfortable.)* Um, I didn't really read the e-mail. I just figured, since our Sunday school teacher was gone for the summer, we didn't need to think about her.

Mr. Wittie: Well, I'm glad to be teaching in Miss Bassett's place this summer. And this service project goes right along with our lesson. God gave us leaders to help us grow closer to Him. And Miss Bassett has helped you all grow close to God through her teaching this past year.

Varsha: She really has. She's a fun teacher.

Stephanie: I like her too, but she's not here.

Austin: That's why we're sending this care package. One thing she taught us is that by serving others, we can serve God.

Varsha: Yeah, we're helping her ministry there by sending this.

Stephanie: *(Picks up items from the table to look at them.)* You're right. These would be great for Miss Bassett to have at the summer camp to help those kids learn about Jesus.

Mr. Wittie: So will you join us?

Stephanie: *(Looks sad.)* But I didn't bring anything to put in! Now I've missed my chance.

Varsha: That's okay, Stephanie. You can help us put in the things the rest of us brought.

*(**Kids** put the rest of the items in the box as **Stephanie** watches.)*

Stephanie: I just thought of something I can put in the box. When my mom was really sick this spring, Miss Bassett prayed for her—a lot. It made me feel a lot better, and my mom ended up getting better too.

Austin: You're going to put your mom in the box?

Stephanie: *(Laughing.)* No. I'm going to put prayers in the box. They'll be invisible, but they'll be there. That's something important Miss Bassett taught me.

Mr. Wittie: Stephanie, that's a great idea! *(**Mr. Wittie** and the **kids** hold hands in a circle around the table and bow their heads for a few moments of silent prayer.)* Amen. *(All look up, smiling.)* Stephanie, why don't you e-mail Miss Bassett that her care package has been filled up with prayers?

Stephanie: Okay, Mr. Wittie. And I'm going to do it as soon as I get home—before I turn on the game!

*(**Mr. Wittie** picks up the box and all exit.)*

Curtain Call

- **In what ways did Miss Bassett help her class grow closer to Jesus?** *(She taught them to serve others, to pray, etc.)* **How about Mr. Wittie?** *(He organized the care package, helping them to serve.)*

- **How is their example like our Bible story?** *(The Bible teaches that Christian leaders should teach us to serve and help us learn about Jesus.)*

- **Who are your Christian leaders, and how have they helped you grow closer to Jesus?** *(Let the kids name Christian leaders they know, and encourage them to name ways they've grown in their faith or learned about Jesus from them.)*

Topic Index

Scripture Index

Pretty Quick & Easy Bible Dramas